The Netsuke
of Japan

The Netsuke of Japan

Legends, History, Folklore and Customs

By Egerton Ryerson

CASTLE BOOKS ★ NEW YORK

This Edition Published by Arrangement
With A. S. Barnes & Co., Inc.

PREFACE

THE REVIVAL OF interest in Japanese art has led to many requests for a new book on Netsuke. Most works dealing with the subject are out of print, expensive and very difficult to obtain. The few recently published are concerned for the most part with the carvers and their work and have little or nothing to say about the meaning of the subjects depicted. Some knowledge of the fables, folklore and customs of old Japan is essential to the appreciation and enjoyment of the netsuke, as indeed it is of all forms of Japanese art. To throw light on this background is the chief aim of my book, though I hope the introductory section on the history and characteristics of the netsuke may also prove useful. Only a brief selection from a vast field has been possible, as the number of motifs and the variety of their treatment are well nigh inexhaustible. It may well be doubted whether anywhere in the world, or at any period of history, art applied to what is after all an ordinary piece of wearing apparel has produced so much to illustrate the character and daily life of a people, in this case a people whose love of beauty and gift of fertile imagination are outstanding.

I am greatly indebted to the authorities of the British Museum and the Victoria and Albert Museum for their courtesy in affording facilities for photographing specimens from their large and valuable collections.

My warm thanks are also due to many who allowed me to photograph examples from their collections or who have helped with counsel and advice, without which the preparation of this book would not have been possible. I should like specially to mention the following: W. Barrett and Son, Ltd., Mrs. Harry G. Beasley, Miss M. Beasley, F. G. Eldred and K. B. Gardner (British Museum), Glendinning & Co., Ltd., I. E. Hills, Collingwood Ingram, W. Lewis, Mrs. C. Oppenheimer, Mrs. Sah Oved, C. H. Perry, L. A. Luxmore, B. W. Robinson (Victoria and Albert Museum), F. J. Daniels, C. J. Dunn and D. E. Mills (School of Oriental and African Studies), Dr. N. E. Waterfield, W. W. Winkworth.

CONTENTS

COLOR PLATES

The color plates appear as a group following page 32.

Negoro Lacquer. Simple netsuke of a boy.

Negoro Lacquer. Shishi on a rectangular base.

Cluster of gourds and foliage.

Recumbent water buffalo.

Ivory figure of a seated monkey.

Shoki astride a crouching Shishi.

Recumbent Shishi.

Frogs on a snail shell, signed Ransen.

Frogs under the moon carrying a lantern.

No dancer in pearl and ivory inlay.

Black lacquer box netsuke.

Ivory *manju*, signed Shibayama.

Shitan wood: gold lacquer carp.

Quails and millet.

Chicken squatting with tail erect.

Foreigners represented by a standing figure of an Eggtester.

Poetess Ono Komachi.

Ghost subject.

Tonkotsu, tobacco box.

Ball-shaped netsuke.

Driftwood netsuke.

Netsuke styled on a Chinese crystal ball.

Recumbent Shishi in ivory.

Monkey with huge peach.

Recumbent water buffalo.

Traveller resting beside his horse.

Stagshorn carved as a Kappa.

Shishi on an openwork garden stool.

Walrus ivory mask on an Oni.

Red Lacquer Mask of a Demon.

Ebony mask of Hannya.

Tiger with raised paw.

Typical Tiger subject.

Young maiden resisting the advances of an octopus.

Square solid Manju.

Box netsuke in gold fundame lacquer.

Haliotis carved as a Kiku.

Ivory figure of Raiden the Thunder Kami.

MONOCHROME PLATES

'Whoever wishes to study Japanese Art, must not fail to devote particular attention to the Netsukes.'

Official Report of Vienna Exhibition, 1922

'No objects of Art found in Japan are more essentially Japanese.'

Japan, by Captain F. Brinkley

'The designs of the Netsuke-Carvers embrace the whole range of Japanese motives and the artist tells his story with the utmost lucidity.'

William Anderson, formerly Keeper of
Oriental Antiquities, British Museum

'Enthusiasts assert that a first-rate netsuke has no rivals. This praise is perhaps not too high if we take care to emphasise the word "first-rate".'

Japan and its Art, by M. Huish

'It is the resource of the carvers in contriving to convey so much in so little that astonishes us, the audacity with which themes for monumental groups are smilingly brought within the compass of an inch or two, with touches of humour, or downright rollicking farce, that belittle the great dramas of history or the fearsome monsters of legend.'

J. Hillier, in *The Antique Collector*, April 1956

'Few people are indifferent to the exquisitely finished details of netsuke or to the quaint and peculiar mode of treating their subjects. To those who possess a certain amount of knowledge of Japanese history, folklore, etc., the interest is enormously increased, for nearly every piece represents some well-known incident, or has a symbolic meaning.'

Netsuke, the M. Tomkinson Collection, by E. Gilbertson

I

Netsuke and Their Makers

WHAT IS A NETSUKE?

A *Netsuke* (pronounced nets'ké, the *u* being almost silent) is a carved or decorated object of wood, ivory or other material, used in old Japan to attach to the girdle (*obi*) small articles in daily use. The suspended articles (called *sagemono* or *koshisage*) included medicine cases (*inrō*) [Pl. 1, *1*], tobacco pouches [Pl. 1, *2*], tinder boxes, purses, drinking gourds, scent bottles, writing materials, seals, keys, etc.

Originally netsuke were probably unornamented as the word itself suggests, being a compound of *ne* a 'root' and *tsuke* 'to fasten'. Any piece of root, stick or bone would have sufficed. The netsuke, with a cord or cords attached, was passed under the girdle from below and protruding over the top acted as a toggle to prevent the cord from slipping [Pl. 4, *2*].

The netsuke were not primarily works of art, but pieces of ordinary wearing apparel. That a nation of artists like the Japanese should make them into beautiful shapes is not surprising when we remember how they apply their amazing instinct for beauty of form and colour in the ornamentation of all the utensils of everyday life. In Japan even a bath towel may be a work of art.

HISTORY OF NETSUKE

Of the early use of this simple device, no historical or pictorial record has yet been found, nor is it likely to be, as chroniclers generally think it unnecessary to record the humble things with which they are most familiar. In the great museum at Nara where there is a large collection of articles in common use during the 8th to 10th Centuries A.D. there are no netsuke. In some medieval pictures gourds and other articles are shown attached to the hilt of the sword which the wearer thrust through his girdle.

Our first acquaintance with the netsuke, as we know it, is related to the emergence of three fashions in dress, the carrying of *inrō*, tobacco pouches and ornamental purses. The first of these arose towards the end of the 16th Century among men of the aristocratic classes who began carrying small cases called *inrō* (*in*, a seal, and *ro*, 'container'). The use of the seal had come from China where it had long been used as a substitute for a signature, or as a means of attesting its genuineness. In addition to carrying the seal and red pigment, the inro came to be used as a receptacle for aromatic herbs and medicines considered pleasant or stimulating. For this purpose the inro was made in three to five compartments neatly fitted together one on top of the other, measuring three or four inches wide, four or five inches long and about half an inch thick. These were held together by two cords which passed up the sides through small holes at the ends of the segments. These cords were then passed through a bead called an *ojime* which kept the segments together, and from thence they went to the netsuke, to which they were fastened in various ways. As a means of carrying the inro, the netsuke served two purposes much appreciated by the wearer. When required, it could easily and quickly be detached; also it enabled the wearer to display his inro with advantage for the admiration of his friends.

And well he might wish to do so, for the lavish skill of the artist and the lacquerer in the decoration of inro has placed them in the front rank of the many beautiful forms of Japanese applied art. The netsuke and the ojime were ornamented to accord with the beauty of inro.

The second fashion came about at the beginning of the 17th Century with the introduction of tobacco into Japan. In spite of efforts on the part of the Government to suppress it, smoking soon became general. At first the habit was confined to the house and for a long time it was considered highly improper for a Samurai to be seen smoking out of doors. It was the artisans and merchants who led the way in outdoor smoking. They found the netsuke, already in use with the inro, a convenient way of carrying their tobacco pouches, pipe cases and tinder boxes or bags. Women smoked as well as men but did not adopt the netsuke as it would have been difficult for them to slip it under their broad sashes. Between the folds of these they were able to insert their pouches, small folding fans and toilet requisites. They also used their capacious sleeves to hold light articles.

Thirdly, in the luxurious Genroku Period (1688-1704) rich merchants strove to emulate the aristocrats with their inro, by wearing elaborately ornamented purses (kinchaku) attached to their girdles by netsuke. These purses were doubtless worn at a much earlier period but as to whether or not this was with netsuke is unknown. In days when common folk employed strings of cash in their financial dealings—the cash was a coin of low value with a hole in the centre*—it was only the very rich who used purses to carry coins of precious metal or gold dust. This form of purse eventually gave way to a wallet carried in the bosom. The word kinchaku, however, has been retained for small bags worn by children, containing identification tablets and amulets.

By the beginning of the 19th Century, the netsuke had become a necessary part of the male dress of all classes of society. As already mentioned it was used as a support for many things besides the inro, the tobacco pouch and the purse. Sometimes several articles were attached to one netsuke. In other cases each had its own.

After the Restoration in 1868 the use of the netsuke declined. This was partly because the wearing of inro went out of fashion; also because of the introduction of the cigarette. Besides, the pouch was now often attached to a wooden pipe case thrust through the girdle, thus rendering the netsuke unnecessary. Finally, there was the widespread adoption of western dress which supplied plenty of pockets.

Makers and dealers in netsuke, however, now discovered a new market for their wares among the many people in America and Europe ready to buy them as curios or ornaments, attracted by their beauty or quaintness. Large quantities were exported including many of the finest specimens, but also many poor and shoddy pieces. To meet the foreign demand a new form of netsuke began to be produced, elaborately carved often with wonderful skill, but by its shape, with sharp projections, likely to catch the clothing, and because of its fragility, quite unsuitable for its original purpose. These are really okimono ('place things'), i.e. ornaments to be put on a shelf, not netsuke to be worn.

In this connection it should be noted that whereas okimono were never meant to be worn some netsuke at least were apparently meant to be used as ornaments. This is suggested in two types, those in which a figure or figures stand on a flat base [Pl. 15, 6], and those in which the centre of gravity has been so designed that they will balance on a very small base, for example on one foot of a dancer [Pl. 4, 5].

MATERIALS

WOOD. The majority of netsuke are of wood [Pl. 4, 3], many kinds being used. The earliest were made of hinoki (Japanese Cypress) prized for its sweet odour and fine texture, but too soft to wear well. Most widely used was tsuge (box-wood) which is hard and fine grained and therefore suitable for minute carving. It also takes a beautiful polish. Many other woods were used, ebony, cherry, persimmon, camphor, camellia, etc. Bamboo was also used.

Wood netsuke were frequently stained, polished or lacquered, either in colour or in gold leaf. One type was decorated with water colour. Occasionally parts were inlaid with ivory, coral or mother-of-pearl or glass (Shibayama Ware).

IVORY. After wood, the most widely used material was ivory, the texture of which lends itself to carving with minute and delicate detail. Ivory had been imported from the 17th Century onwards having first been used to make plectra for musical instruments. Its soft smooth surface makes it pleasant to handle, and the lustre, colour and grain markings add to its beauty. Tusks of animals other than elephants, such as the wild boar, narwhal and hippopotamus, were also used. Ivory netsuke are frequently pyramidal in shape probably because this was the most economical way of cutting the tusks.

* Pl. 40, 4

PLATE 1

1. Netsuke, with bead, *ojime*, and Medicine Case,
*inro. B.M.**

2. Netsuke, with bead, tobacco pouch and pipe case.
V & A†

* British Museum, London, W.C.1
† Victoria and Albert Museum, London, S.W.7.

HORN. Though not as suitable as ivory, horn was sometimes substituted, being more easily obtained.

BONE. This was used, but there was always the difficulty of finding solid pieces suitable in size and thickness.

Other substances used were fruit stones, nut shells, amber, tortoise shell, sea shells, mother-of-pearl [Pl. 22], stones, metal [Pl. 2], crystal, rattan [Pl. 3], enamel ware and porcelain [Pl. 4].

In later netsuke, materials were sometimes combined, the body of a man, for instance, being made of wood and his head of ivory.

FORMS

MANJŪ netsuke. The simplest and probably the earliest form is that of a button one to three inches in diameter, known as *manjū* from its resemblance to a Japanese rice cake or bun of that name. Though generally circular it is sometimes oval or rectangular. It was ornamented by incision, high or low relief, (*uki-bori*) [Pl. 2, *1*], or deeply undercut (*sukashi-bori*) [Pl. 2, *3*], The cord was fastened in various ways. Either it was passed through two holes (*himotōshi*) close together and connected by a 'V'-shaped channel; or it was inserted through one hole on the bottom and tied to a stopper or to the inside of a detachable portion of the netsuke, thus rendering the knot invisible. Or in some cases it was tied to a metal ring. In rare instances chains were used [Pl. 4, *6*].

'MIRROR LID'. A variant of the *manjū* is the *kagami-buta*, or 'mirror lid' netsuke, in which a metal disc, bearing some resemblance in shape to the round Japanese mirror was inserted in a depression on one side. Ornamentation was incised, and often inlaid with precious metals, or was hammered in repoussé work [Pl. 2, *5*]. This work was carried out by goldsmiths and other metal workers [Pl. 22, *6*].

STATUETTES. The most common and finest type is that of the sculptured statuette or group of figures (called *katabori*) [Pl. 3]. The shape was generally determined by the object represented, but carvers showed a remarkable capacity for posing their subjects to form a compact mass, pleasant to handle. The cord was usually attached through two holes (*himotōshi*) connected by a 'V'-shaped channel as with manjū netsuke. In good netsuke these were placed so that the subject might be displayed to the best advantage. Frequently, to hide the knot, one hole was made slightly larger than the other. The holes were sometimes lined with an ivory or bone ring to prevent wear. In certain cases the holes were dispensed with, the cord passing through an opening in the carving.

THE SEAL FORM [Pl. 3]. This has a figure, often a *shishi* (Chinese lion) mounted on a rectangular or cylindrical base. Some of the earliest of this type were actually seals imported from China. The Chinese seal form was imitated by Japanese craftsmen with, of course, their own variations. The signature engraved on the bottom of the base in a special form of writing (*tensho*) [Pl. 3] was either omitted or some felicitous phrase like 'Happiness and Long Life' substituted.

CLAM SHELL. Ivory netsuke in the shape of a clam shell with the mouth partly opened [Pl. 3], afforded the maker the opportunity of carving within, protected from rough handling, scenes of exquisite delicacy.

MASKS. From early times masks were worn by performers in certain dances, religious and secular, and many ancient specimens have been preserved in temples and as heirlooms in aristocratic families. They were not worn by actors, as many have supposed, except in the dance interludes in the drama. 'The sculptor possessed great skill in the delineation of the human countenance under the influence of emotion. . . . It is difficult to conceive any type of face, any display of passion, any exhibition of affection, of fury, of cruelty, of benevolence, of voluptuousness, of imbecility, that these masks do not reproduce with remarkable realism.'*

Carvers of masks [Pl. 28] sometimes made miniature specimens to show their skill, or turned them into netsuke by supplying at the back a bridge to support the cord [Pl. 28]. The most famous makers of netsuke masks were the Deme family, of whom Deme Uman in the 18th Century produced work of the finest quality. To his signature he added the boast 'first under heaven' (*ten ka ichi*), a practice often followed by other members of his family less skilled. Netsuke made up [Pl. 3] of groups of masks are fairly common.

SASHI netsuke. Another form is the *sashi* netsuke [Pl. 4], a rod six to eight inches in length with the cord hole at the upper end. It was thrust under the girdle from above.

* *Japan*, Vol. VII, Captain Brinkley.

A similar form is the *hasami* netsuke, which was clipped on the girdle.

HYŌTAN (Gourds). Dried gourds used as water or wine bottles and small ones as scent bottles, were among the 'hanging things' attached to the girdle by netsuke. A small gourd was itself sometimes used as a netsuke. Also netsuke made in the shape of these small gourds or of the gourd scent bottle (*nioi bin*) are not uncommon [Pl. 4].

SAISHIKI netsuke (*saishiki*—colour) [Pl. 4] are brilliantly coloured figurines of very light wood, made in large quantities during the early part of the 19th Century in Nara and hence termed *Nara ningyō* (*ningyō*—doll). They were frequently rough cut in the style known as 'sculpture à facettes' or in Japanese as *ittō-bori*. Resembling the work of the famous 18th-Century carver Shūzan they generally bear his signature. The great carver in fact never signed his work.

ICHIRAKU netsuke are woven with slender rattan or wire (Pl. 3, 6).

TRICK AND TOY netsuke [Pl. 3, 7]. Trick netsuke were made in many clever ways, loose seeds of the lotus pod, or a worm slipping in and out of a rotten pear, and yet in some mysterious way securely fastened; long necks and protruding tongues of goblins which slide when the netsuke is tilted; movable jaws on skulls and many other amusing devices.

SUIGARA AKE, or Ashtray netsuke [Pl. 2], in the form of a metal or wooden cup, supplied a need in addition to that of supporting the tobacco pouch. The Japanese pipe only holds a pinch of tobacco about the size of a pea. When the smoker has taken two or three whiffs he must empty and refill. Indoors he used a bamboo receptacle (*haifuki*) in the tobacco box into which to knock his pipe. Out-of-doors the ashtray netsuke was a handy article. Into it he emptied his pipe, then refilled and lighted his new pipeful on the smouldering ashes of the discarded wad of tobacco.

SIGNATURES

The Japanese learnt their method of writing from the Chinese in the 5th and 6th Centuries A.D. Prior to that time, as far as is known, they had no script of their own. Unfortunately the ideographs, being symbols of ideas, not phonetic signs, were ill adapted for the transcription of a language so different from the Chinese in the form of words, in grammar and in syntax. Many headaches and much time and labour would have been saved, had the Japanese invented or borrowed an alphabet. The one redeeming feature has been that the use of the brush in transcribing these complicated symbols has demanded a skill and dexterity which has contributed in no small measure to the development of Japanese art. The Chinese characters by themselves proved inadequate and in the 9th Century the Japanese invented a system of phonetic signs representing forty-seven syllables known as *kana*. This syllabic nomenclature exists in two forms, with some variants, *katakana* written with straight or angular lines and *hiragana*, a cursive style. Kana is used to represent particles, the endings of words and small words. Only rarely is it found on netsuke. Here signatures were written in two or more characters, with the possible addition of a seal, in special seal script (*tensho*) or a 'written seal' (*kakihan*), which is a kind of trade-mark. Deciphering signatures is not at all an easy matter. There is the problem of reading. This may be according to the Japanese (*kun*), or according to Sino-Japanese reading (*on*). For instance, the carver Tamikuni (*kun*) more often has his name read Minkoku (*on*). That is not all. Several people whose names are written with different characters may have them read alike. There are two Minkoku's with different characters for *koku*.

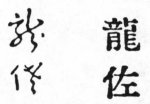

Specimen of a difficult signature

RYŪSA
as engraved on netsuke
in 'grass writing' *sōsho*

RYŪSA
as printed in *kaisho*

Added to these difficulties is the greater one of knowing what the characters actually are. This is fairly simple when they are written in the *kaisho* style with every stroke of the brush carved in full (though even here there may be puzzling abbreviations), but much harder to decipher when written in the cursive *Sōsho* or 'grass writing', in which an elaborate character may be reduced to one or two wriggly lines. In many cases even an educated Japanese may be stumped. The signatures are a

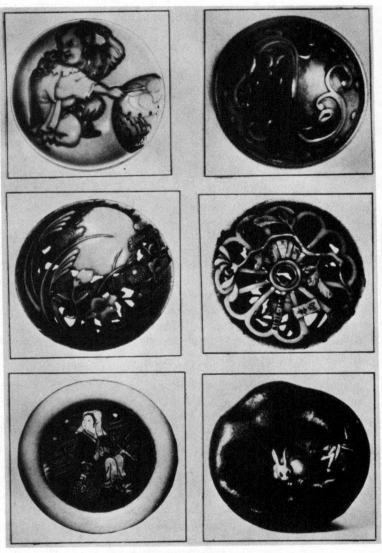

PLATE 2: VARIETIES OF NETSUKE

1. Manjū (*uki-bori*).   V & A
3. Manjū undercut (*sukashi-bori*)
5. Mirror Netsuke, *kagami-buta*. Ohara-me, woman of Ohara village.

2. Ashtray, *suigaraake*. Metal. V & A
4. Back of No. 3
6. Manjū. Iron with gold inlay

fascinating study for those who have acquired a fair knowledge of Japanese writing or have an abundant supply of time and patience. Most collectors, however, will be satisfied if they can manage to memorise the signatures of a few of the better-known carvers.

AGE AND GENUINENESS OF NETSUKE

The age and the genuineness of the signature of a netsuke is often difficult to determine with any degree of certainty, for there is no branch of Japanese art in which more copying, honest and dishonest, has been perpetrated. It was the normal practice of apprentices and pupils to copy the work of their masters in order to improve their own skill, and also to make objects for sale. The master often conferred on the pupil the honour of using his signature, or the signature indicated merely that the netsuke was the work of the house or firm and not any particular member of it. There was, of course, nothing dishonest in this. But there have been many clever forgers in Japan, as in western lands, a fact pointed out as early as A.D. 1781 by the author of the *Sōken Kishō*. Much skill and experience is called for to assess the age and genuineness of a netsuke. The expert may note the signs of wear caused by rubbing against the clothes or the abrasion of the holes by the friction of the cord. Yet an old piece may show little signs of wear, because it has been seldom used or carefully looked after, whereas a modern one may have been much worn and roughly handled. The bleaching of the parts exposed to the light is regarded as a sign of age. But the forger knows many ways of simulating these marks of antiquity. The skill and style of workmanship of a carver are points which help the expert.

The choice of subjects is also some indication of age. Netsuke elaborately carved with projections which might catch the clothing can without doubt be declared modern. Between 1800 and 1850 portrayal of the lowlier forms of animal life, such as rats, snakes, snails and frogs was popular.

In the 18th Century when workmanship was generally cruder, the subjects were for the most part seals, grotesque monsters and *sennin* (see p. 20).

The uncertainty as to age and genuineness may be very discouraging to those who put pride of possession above everything else; it is less disturbing for those who value chiefly beauty and charm, or clever, interesting and amusing examples of the artist's skill.

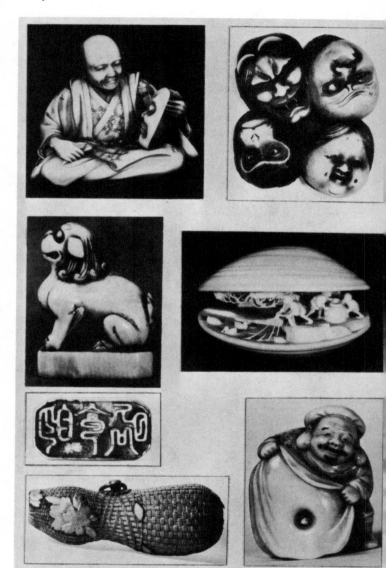

PLATE 3: VARIETIES OF NETSUKE

1. Statuette, *katabori*. Mask Carver. H. 1½″.   *B.M.*
3. Seal. Dog of Fo. H. 2″.
5. Base of seal. (Seal style of writing, *tensho*)
6. Ichiraku. Finely woven reeds. L. 1⅞″.

2. Square Manjū. Group of Masks. H. 2½″.
4. Clam Shell (protecting delicate carving). Cormorant fishers. H. 1⅜″.
7. Trick Netsuke. Disappearing rat in Daikoku's bag. H. 2¼″.   *B.M.*

FAMOUS CARVERS

The makers of netsuke are seldom mentioned in Japanese literature on the Arts, doubtless largely because of the inferior social position they occupied, being for the most part artisans and consequently looked down upon by the literary and official class to which most painters belonged. For a long time they carried on their work as a side line, their main occupation being the carving of images, masks, puppets or dolls. Some were amateurs, making netsuke as a hobby. The earliest definite information is in a book on sword furniture by Inaba Michitatsu entitled *Sōken Kishō*, published in Osaka in 1781. The author, a well-informed merchant of antiques, of refined taste, gives brief particulars of about fifty-seven netsuke carvers of his day, as well as some artistic criticism of their work. Most of those mentioned lived in Osaka, Kyoto and Edo (Tokyo).

Pride of place is given to Tosa Mitsuoki, better known by his art name Shūzan, who died in 1691. A note by his son is quoted as follows, 'My father who is artistically known as Hōgen Shūzan, was called Mitsuoki or Tansenso, and enjoyed a high reputation as a painter. He was very fond of carving and loved to reproduce, with due alteration of enlargement or reduction, the quaintest and most unusual figures shown in the Sankaikyō (Classic of the Mountain and the Ocean) or the Ressenden (Lives of the Rishi). In fact, any figure he fancied took shape under his chisel. His scheme of colouring was so excellent that ordinary folks can have no conception of it. But as he ceased to carve after reaching middle life his works are very scarce and of correspondingly high value.'

Shūzan worked in *hinoki* (cypress), a soft light wood, which together with the colouring lacked permanence. Netsuke reputed to be his survive but their genuineness is, to say the least, doubtful. He did not sign his work, but many imitations bearing his signature exist, particularly the coloured figurines made in Nara (cf. p. 14).

Among the carvers mentioned in the *Sōken Kishō* specially noteworthy are Miwa, Masanao, Tomotada and Ryūsa. Miwa, who had been a carver of temple images, began with large netsuke of soft wood, depicting hermits, goblins and grotesque creatures, but later used close-grained cherry wood to portray characters to be seen in the everyday life of the streets. He was a pioneer in lining the cord openings with rims of horn or ivory to prevent erosion. His signature was usually placed on the soles of the feet of his figures.

Of Masanao, the *Sōken Kishō* says, 'His skill in carving was

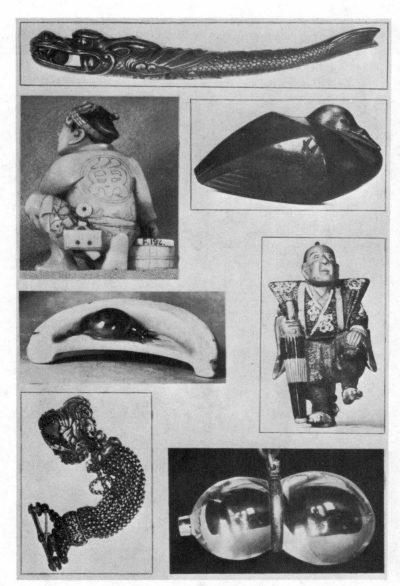

PLATE 4: VARIETIES OF NETSUKE

1. Sashi Netsuke. Flying Dragon. L. 6¾″
2. How a Netsuke was worn. (Back of Fishmonger of Pl. 35, 1)
3. Boldly cut wood. (*itto bori*). Duck. L. 1¾″
4. Porcelain. Snail on potsherd. L. 3½″. B.M.
5. Coloured wood, *Saishiki*, also called *Nara Ningyo*. Dancer. H. 2½″   V & A
6. Silver. Chains used instead of cord. L. 4″.
7. Crystal. Gourd, or scent bottle shape.

great. He worked in both ivory and wood and his productions are much prized.' His animals and toy sparrows are much prized to-day, though few originals survive. 'The charm of his netsuke lies in their striking originality of design, bold outlines, free subtle curves, smooth surfaces unmarred by extraneous detail, and spirited character.'*

* *The Art of the Netsuke Carver*, F. Meinertzhagen.

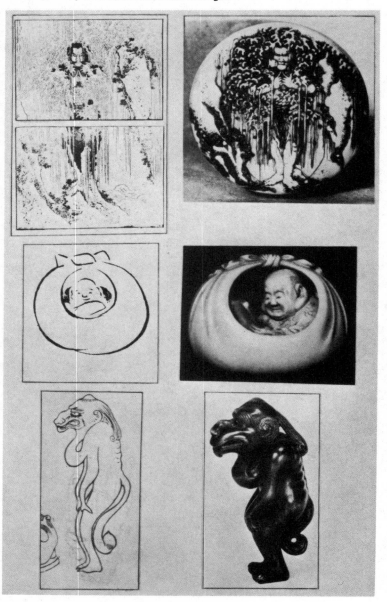

Tomotada is specially noted for his recumbent figure of an ox, of which there are many imitations. He also carved *kirin*, stags, horses, wolves and tigers, mostly in ivory. In his day he was greatly admired.

'Ryūsa,' says the *Sōken Kishō*, 'was a turner by profession. He showed remarkable skill in making round netsuke, which were lathe turned, and particularly suitable for gold lacquer inro, because the lacquer received no injury from contact with the netsuke.' His name is given to deeply undercut netsuke, of which he is reputed to be the inventor.

Onagi Senzō, a farmer, who lived in Shibayama, Chiba Prefecture, in the late 18th Century, devised a method of wood carving inlaid with shell and other materials. Netsuke and objects ornamented in this way are known as Shibayama ware.

Ogasawara Issai (also late 18th Century) has been regarded by some as the greatest of all netsuke carvers. His minute carving in ivory and whale tusk won such admiration that his netsuke were difficult to obtain even in his lifetime.

Ikkwan was a priest of the middle of the 19th Century who specialised in his early days in carving sleeping *shōjō* (drunken sprites) and later rats, for which he is specially famed.

Another great carver of the 19th Century was Hōjitsu or Meikeisai, an independent craftsman, whose work was refined, realistic and elaborate.

Kwaigyoku Masatsugu (1812–1892), 'a wizard among netsuke carvers',* used wood, ivory, amber and tortoise shell. Beginning with simple designs, his work became more and more elaborate. His netsuke became so popular that he employed pupils who used his signature but whose craftsmanship was frequently unworthy of their master.

Of most of the 2,500 netsuke makers recorded little is known beyond their names, approximate date, locality and the material with which they worked.†

* Op. cit., Meinertzhagen.
† Those wishing further information on this subject should consult *The Art of the Netsuke Carver* by F. Meinertzhagen, and *Netsuke* by Y. Okada.

PLATE 5: EXAMPLES OF COPYING

1. Illustration in 'Yehon Sakigake' by Hokusai, A.D. 1836. Mongaku under Waterfall.

2. Manjū Netsuke of Mongaku. B.M.

3. Illustration in 'Keisai Riako Gwashi'. A.D. 1797

4. Netsuke of Hotei in bag.

5. Illustration in 'Soken Kisho' A.D. 1781.

6. Mythical Animal. H. 2¼″

SUBJECTS

The range and variety of the subjects portrayed in the netsuke is indeed vast. Gods, demons, ghosts, strange mythical creatures, animals, birds, fish, flowers and other natural objects, realistic genre representations of daily life, warriors, dancers, musicians, acrobats and wrestlers, illustrations of stories from Chinese and Japanese history and folklore, fairy tales and novels, objects strange or commonplace, etc. The list might be extended indefinitely.

The various ways in which these motives were depicted sprang for the most part from the keen observation and fertile imagination of the carvers, though occasionally we find a carver borrowing an idea from the work of a famous painter or from one of the picture books so popular at the time, or more rarely we come across instances of direct copying [Pl. 5].

A comparison with other forms of Japanese art reveals the frequency with which the same motives were used by painters, lacquerers and metal workers alike.

From the subjects chosen and the method of their interpretation we may infer something of the character of carvers and of the people for whom they worked. This may be summarised as follows:

1. A great love of nature, with particular affection for lower forms of animal and vegetable life.
2. A keen sense of humour.
3. A liking of anything quaint, odd or grotesque.
4. Great interest in the simple things of everyday life.
5. A love of stories, especially queer stories.
6. A light-hearted amusement in erotic suggestion.*

CLEANING NETSUKE

Wooden and lacquer netsuke may be cleaned with turpentine, not water, using a soft camel-hair brush.

The cleaning of ivory netsuke will vary according to the condition or form. Plain surfaces may be dry cleaned with a soft rubber or kneadable eraser. Dirt may be removed from carved and reticulated work by means of a camel-hair brush soaked in alcohol. If the dirt is difficult to remove a little water may be mixed with the spirit, but water should be avoided if possible. When cleaned the netsuke should be wiped dry.

Tarnished metal-ware may be brightened with liquid ammonia, but care should be taken to protect ivory or lacquer parts.

---

* Standards of taste in this matter vary in different countries and have fluctuated considerably in our own through the ages. In netsuke the erotic is usually suggested in a form which to the uninitiated would pass unobserved. It must be admitted that a few are unequivocally pornographic but there is no exploitation of the nude in the interests of lasciviousness. Indeed, though beauty and force of line constitute the Japanese artist's special excellence, he seems to have been strangely uninterested in the exquisite curves of the female form. Portrayal of the nude is conspicuous by its rarity in netsuke as in other forms of Japanese art.

2

Chinese Stories

FROM THE INTRODUCTION of Chinese civilisation in the 6th Century A.D. to the Restoration in 1868, the Japanese people were under the influence of Chinese thought, which arrived in many successive waves. As a result everyone, from the most educated to the most illiterate, became familiar with certain outstanding facts of Chinese history as well as a great mass of legend and folklore. Among these, Japanese artists, painters, potters and metal workers found innumerable interesting subjects. The netsuke carvers were not slow to take advantage of this vast field of attractive and amusing material, though of course only a certain portion lent itself to portrayal by the carver's knife.

Confusion sometimes arises from variants of a story and because sometimes the same story is told of two different people. Chinese celebrities are often known by several names, their personal names, their literary name, a nickname, or an official title.

1. SENNIN AND OTHER MYTHOLOGICAL CHARACTERS

SENNIN (Sanscrit: Rishi). They play a part in the mystic scenes of Buddhism and Taoism and are described as beings who enjoy rest (i.e. exemption from transmigration) in the solitude of mountains for a hundred thousand years, after the lapse of which time they again enter the circle of transmigration. They must guard their thoughts against any carnal affection which would deprive them of their status. They are generally regarded as magicians with supernatural powers.

So many and varied are netsuke of Sennin and so inconsistent were carvers in attaching attributes that identification is in many cases exceedingly difficult.

CHINNAN (Chinese: Ch'ennan), also called *Suikyo* and *Nan Boku*. This Sennin is sometimes depicted with a bowl or gourd from which emerges a dragon, or riding across a stream on his hat. Generally, however, he appears as a beggar with long hair, dressed in mugwort leaves, and leaning upon a stick. By his magic power, he was able to travel thousands of miles a day. His food was dog's flesh and his occupation making baskets, transmuting metals and preparing magic pills. One day, passing through a village, he saw people praying for rain which the parched ground showed to be sorely needed. In a bed of dried mud he detected the presence of a dragon and, thrusting in his stick, compelled him to come out and open the flood gates of heaven, thus putting an end to the drought.

CHOKWARŌ AND HIS MULE [Pl. 6, 2]. Chokwarō, one of the immortals of the Taoists, is said to have lived about the end of the 7th Century A.D. The Emperor had invited him to Court to accept priestly office and the hand of a princess, together with the honour of having his portrait hung in the Hall of Ancestors, but all these honours he declined as he preferred a wandering life in company with his magic mule or horse. This animal carried him thousands of miles a day without food and required no stabling as at night he shrivelled up inside his master's gourd. When required next morning, all Chokwarō had to do was to spit into the gourd and out came the mule, soon assuming life size and ready for the day's journey. Probably, this story accounts for the Japanese proverb 'a pony from a gourd', meaning a surprisingly unexpected event.

Sometimes Chokwarō is represented with his mule and gourd, sometimes the gourd alone with the mule or horse emerging suggests the tale.

GAMA SENNIN [Pl. 6, 4]. Generally, he is portrayed as a lean fellow without hair on his face but with protuberances on his body and carrying on his shoulder a frog or toad, sometimes three-legged. He seems to have had the power of exhaling his spirit, which, leaving the body devitalised, could roam or return at will. Once it took up its abode in the body of a frog.

Gama compounded magic pills for lengthening life and may be seen sometimes administering one to his companion, the frog.

GYOKUSHI, or GYOKUSHISHO. A Sennin, who had supernatural power over the winds and the rain. He was able to ride for thousands of miles a day on a horse of clay, blowing from his mouth coloured clouds of spray, the drops of which turned into jewels.

IKKAKU [Pl. 6, 1]. The name means 'the one horned'. This magician is generally depicted with a woman on his back.

The scene of the legend is India. Ikkaku's mother was a deer, and hence the horn, while his father was a sage with occult powers, which the son inherited. The story is an unusual one of the fall from grace of a sage honoured for his chastity and piety. The trouble began when, one day, Ikkaku slipped on some wet ground and in his wrath took revenge on the Rain Dragon by shutting him up in a cave, thus causing a drought. The injury to the crops led the king of Benares to consult his astrologers, who informed him that the origin of the trouble must be the occult powers exercised by one of the sages dwelling in the mountains, whose spiritual power would vanish if he were to lose his chastity. They suggested that a beautiful woman be sent to tempt the holy man. The plot succeeded as Ikkaku fell in love with the woman and, infatuated, he offered to accompany her back to Benares.

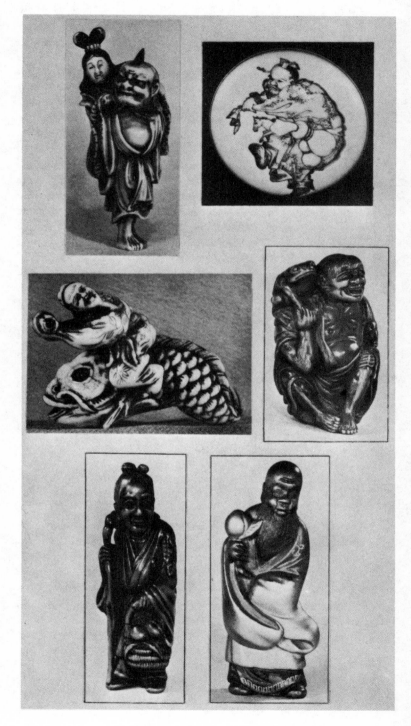

PLATE 6: CHINESE LEGENDS

1. Ikkaku. H. 3″.		2. Chokwarō.	
3. Kinkō. H. 1½″.		4. Gama.	V & A
5. Seiōbo. H. 3″.		6. Tōbōsaku. H. 2½″.	

On the journey, the lady grew weary and he carried her on his back. Little did he suspect the dire punishment that awaited him. Now bereft of his supernatural power, through his fall from grace, he was at the mercy of the king who had no compunction in putting him to death. The spell upon the dragon was broken; the rain fell and the country was saved from any further irresponsible use of magic by the unhappy Ikkaku.

KANZAN (Chinese: Hanshan) and JITTOKU (Chinese: Shihte). Two Sennin usually represented together, Kanzan with a scroll and Jittoku with a broom. They spent most of their time in the kitchen of a monastery speaking what seemed unintelligible gibberish to each other and hurling insults at any visitors who might appear. A legend is told of Jittoku that when crows came and devoured the food set before the guardian deity of the temple Jittoku took a stick and beat the image soundly saying 'If you cannot defend your own food, how can you protect the Temple?' [Pl. 7, 3].

KINKŌ [Pl. 6, 3] rides a large carp. One of the Taoist Immortals, he is said to have lived in the 12th Century spending his days by a stream painting fish and singing songs. One day, the King of the Fishes invited him to visit the regions over which he ruled, and Kinkō, after telling his disciples when he expected to return, dived under the waves. On the day named the disciples assembled in large numbers on the bank and were rewarded by seeing their master returning on the back of a large carp. After admonishing them never to kill fish, the sage once more mounted his carp and disappeared for ever, some say returning to the fishy realm below, and others, mounting to the skies.

KOREIJIN. A Taoist Sennin accompanied by a white tiger.

KOAN. Though his age is given as ten thousand years, he has the appearance of a child with little clothing. He rides upon a long-tailed tortoise, a symbol of longevity.

RASHINJIN was a Chinese hermit to whom came a golden man desiring to be healed. The patient turned out to be a dragon who, in gratitude, carried his doctor off to the skies.

RŌGYOKU. A Sennin who was also a Chinese princess. She accompanied her Imperial sire to the realm of Seiōbo, the Fairy Queen, riding on the back of the sacred Hō-ō bird.

SEIŌBO [Pl. 6, 5] (Chinese: Hsi Wang Mu) is the Chinese Queen of the Fairies, 'The Royal Mother of the West', who dwells in a palace where there is a peach orchard, the fruit in which ripens only every three thousand years and has the power of conferring on any who eats thereof, the gift of immortality. She is portrayed with an attendant carrying a basket of peaches (see Tōbōsaku).

SHIEI is another Immortal who rides a large carp. This was originally a small red fish which he caught one day and, finding it a very pretty specimen, took it home and kept it as a pet in his garden pond. A year passed and to his astonishment his little pet had grown to a fish of prodigious size and had developed wings. This creature now informed Shiei that as a reward for his kindness and care he would take him up to heaven but, as he could only travel through the element of water, they must await a propitious occasion. At last the day came when there was a great torrent of rain and Shiei was translated to the heavenly regions on the back of his beautiful red carp. It is said that he returns to visit the earth every seventy years.

TEKKAI. One of the Immortals of the Taoists, Tekkai, like Gama, had the power of exhaling his spirit. As a youth he was a man of 'commanding stature and dignified mien', who received instruction from no less a person than the great Rōshi (Laotse) himself. For his lessons he was sometimes summoned to heaven, at other times Rōshi descended to earth. He told his disciple that, should he exhale his spirit, he must watch his body carefully for if left for more than seven days it would vanish. It happened on one occasion Tekkai was called to go in spirit to the death bed of his mother, and remaining too long, returned to find his body gone. The corpse of a lame beggar was lying by the roadside and into this Tekkai entered, continuing his existence as a poor philosopher who hobbled about leaning on an iron staff [Pl. 8, 3].

TŌBŌSAKU [Pl. 6, 6] (Chinese: Tung Fang So). A magician who, after a number of reincarnations, is said to have appeared at the court of Butei in A.D. 138 and instructed him in magic and superstitious rites.

The Emperor once saw a green sparrow and asked Tōbōsaku what it portended, to which the reply was that it was an omen foretelling the coming of Seiōbo, the Fairy Queen. Shortly afterwards she arrived with seven of her magic peaches and, while she was eating one, she noticed Tōbōsaku watching her through a window. She exclaimed 'That man stole three of my peaches and is now three thousand years old'.

Tōbōsaku is represented carrying a peach, an emblem of longevity.

2. LEGENDS AND HISTORY

BASHIKŌ (Chinese: Ma Shih Huang). A Chinese physician, who specialised in the treatment of horses, is supposed to have lived in the time of the Emperor Huang Ti (Jap. Kōtei) 2968 B.C.

There is a legend that he cured a sick dragon by performing acupuncture on its throat.

KYOYŪ and SŌFU. Two sages who lived in the semi-mythological period of Chinese history about 2350 B.C. When the Emperor suggested to his counsellor Kyoyū that he might abdicate in his favour, the sage declined and went to a waterfall nearby to wash his ears defiled by such worldly temptation. His companion Sōfu, hearing of this, immediately washed his ears and eyes too, and seeing his ox drinking lower down the stream, led him away lest the beast also might be contaminated.

GOSHISHO, a Chinese General (c. 500 B.C.) [Pl. 7, 2]. When the King of Wu wanted a new counsellor, he decreed it must be a man of great physical strength and literary ability. Candidates for the post were required to hold aloft with one hand an iron kettle weighing over one thousand pounds and to write answers to three difficult questions with the other hand. Goshisho won and is often portrayed performing this feat.

KIKUJIDŌ, 'The chrysanthemum boy', an attendant of the Chinese Emperor Boku-Ō, of the Chow dynasty (c. 950 B.C.). For inadvertently touching the cushion on which his master was resting he was sent into exile. Before leaving the court, the Emperor taught him certain mystic words received from the Buddha (who according to Chinese chronology died 949 B.C.). Kikujidō went to a distant valley where chrysanthemums grew in profusion and passed the time writing the magic words on the leaves and casting them into a stream. When picked up by those who lived lower down the stream these leaves were found to impart power and allay hunger and thirst. Water used to wash off the writing became an elixir of everlasting youth.

PLATE 7: CHINESE LEGENDS AND HISTORY

1. Kanshin. H. 1⅜″.	B.M.	2. Goshisho. H. 2″.	B.M.
3. Kanzan and Jittoku.		4. Hankwai. H. 2″.	V & A
5. Ōgishi.	B.M.	6. Yojō. H. 1½″.	B.M.

HENJAKU (Chinese: Pien Ts'iao). This is the title of a famous physician of the 6th Century B.C. He began life as an innkeeper. One day he received a visit from a sage and magician named Chosunkun (Chinese, Ch'ang Sang Kun) who, observing his host's unusual attainments, gave him instruction in the practice of medicine. Henjaku proved such an apt pupil that he soon excelled his master. He is said to have been the first to dissect the human body. Even more useful for the art of healing was his possession of a transparent abdomen, enabling him to observe the flow of blood and the action of drugs.

RYŪHŌ (Chinese: Liu Pang), 247-195 B.C. He is shown either holding the magic mirror which revealed not only the outward appearance, but also the inner character of those reflected in it; or else in the act of killing a dragon.

Ryūhō began life as a peasant who, by his efforts to prevent brigandage and help travellers, gained the approval of a wealthy man in the district. This man gave him his daughter in marriage, in this case, as often, the first step in a prosperous career. Popularity came after he had been successful in organising a revolt against the hardships of those employed in the erection of costly palace buildings. Other dissatisfied groups joined him and enabled him to bring about a revolution in the State of Ts'u. The new sovereign appointed him to the command of the southern army, while a rival was put in charge of the northern forces. The two generals had a wager that he who first entered Hsien-Yang, the capital of a province in revolt, should be entitled to become its governor. Ryūhō won the race and gave evidence of his fine character as a ruler by suspending all severe laws, with punishment only for murder, bodily injury and theft. It was here that he acquired the magic mirror described above. Unfortunately rivalries and quarrels led to bloody battles, in some of which Ryūhō suffered heavy losses. In the end, however, thanks largely to the wise strategy of his great comrade, General Chōryō, he overcame his foes and became Emperor of China and founder of the dynasty of Han.

The Three Heroes of the Han Dynasty

CHŌRYŌ, KANSHIN and CHIMPEI were three generals who assisted Ryūhō (Liu Pang) in his wars with rivals, and by their wise counsels helped him to become Emperor of China and founder of the Han dynasty in 206 B.C.

PLATE 8: CHINESE LEGENDS AND HISTORY

1. Chōryō and Kōsekikō.   *2.* Kwanyu. H. 3″.   *B.M.*   *3.* Tekkai.
4. Meikō and Yōkihi.   *V & A*   *5.* Shiba Onkō. H. 1½″.
6. Kakkyo.   *B.M.*   *7.* Mōsō.   *V & A*

CHŌRYŌ and KŌSEKIKŌ (Chinese: Chang Liang and Hwang She Kung) [Pl. 8, *1*]. Chōryō is usually depicted under a bridge, picking up a shoe which he hands to Kōsekikō mounted on a mule. The subject is sometimes caricatured, e.g. with Ebisu and Daikoku, Gods of good luck, acting the parts.

Chōryō, despoiled of his position of Governor of Han, led a wandering life until he eventually joined Ryūhō (Liu Pang). During these wanderings, when crossing a bridge one day, he encountered an old and poor-looking man mounted on a mule who had at that moment the misfortune to drop his shoe in the stream. Chōryō, with great politeness and regardless of the indignity involved, dismounted and picking up the shoe, handed it to the old man, who thereupon gave him an invitation to meet him at a certain place where he would receive some slight recognition of his kindness. Accordingly, Chōryō came to the place on the appointed day but alas not at the appointed hour. The old man told him he must be more punctual if he wanted to receive his reward and gave him another appointment. Once again Chōryō inadvertently showed his disrespect by arriving late. On the third occasion, however, he arrived first and when the old man appeared he revealed the fact that he was none other than Kōsekikō, the Yellow Stone Elder, a sage of great renown. He handed Chōryō a roll of manuscript saying 'He who studies this book will become the teacher of princes'. The book turned out to be one of military strategy of inestimable value to the recipient in his future wars.

Tradition has it that this book was used by Yoshitsune and also by Kusunoki Masashige, two generals famous in Japanese history.

KANSHIN (Chinese: Han Hsin) [Pl. 7, *1*]. The grandson of a prince of Han who had been deprived of his territory, he was reduced to poverty and had to support himself by fishing in the moat of his father's castle. One day he was helped with food by a poor woman engaged in steeping her flax in the water. When he rose to power he remembered this kind act and rewarded it. On another occasion on his way to join the forces of Ryūhō, he passed through a market place where he found his path blocked by a coarse ruffian, who refused to let him pass unless he would either draw sword and fight or else crawl between the braggart's legs. Rather than demean himself by engaging in a vulgar street brawl, he chose the latter alternative in spite of the merriment it caused among onlookers.

CHIMPEI (Chinese: Ch'en P'ing) rose from poverty and obscurity to be one of the three chief ministers of Ryūhō assisting him by his wise counsels and thus contributing to the triumphs which led to the establishment of the Han dynasty.

HANKWAI (Chinese: Fan K'uai) [Pl. 7, *4*]. Originally a low-class dog butcher, he rose to be a minister of Ryūhō, the founder of the Han dynasty in 206 B.C., to whom also he was attached by being related to the Empress. He happened to hear of a plot against the life of Ryūhō and, knowing that the conspirators were in the palace feasting, he forced his way in carrying the door with him. By joining in the revelry and feigning to be drunk, he gave the Emperor an opportunity to escape.

BAIFUKU. Baifuku was carried to heaven on the wings of the Hō-ō or Sacred Bird. He was an official of the Han dynasty, who, having succeeded in his endeavours to bring about political reform, retired to the mountains to meditate and seek the elixir of life. He was rewarded by being translated and centuries later was deified.

SHUBAISHIN. A peasant of the Han dynasty who for his studious habits was appointed the Governor of a province. This was a surprise to his wife who, thinking his reading a waste of time, had deserted him, but now wished to be taken back. She received the brusque reply, 'If you can pick up spilt water, you may return.'

Heroes of the Later Han Dynasty

Three generals living at the end of the 2nd Century A.D.

RYŪBI (Chinese: Liu Pei), also known as Gentoku. Long ears, tall, with hands reaching below his knees.

KWANYU (Chinese: Kuan Yu) [Pl. 8, *2*]. 'The Lord of the Splendid Black Beard' which he strokes. He sometimes carries the brocade bag given him by Ryūbi as a receptacle for the beard. He may be accompanied by retainers, or playing go.

CHŌHI (Chinese: Chang Fei). Flowing hair, fanlike beard. Carries a straight double-edged spear.

All three generals began life in a humble way. Ryūbi, although the descendant of an Emperor, was reduced to poverty at the death of his father, and had to support his mother by making straw shoes and mats.

Kwanyu started as a seller of bean curd, while Chōhi was a butcher and wine merchant. In the days when the House of Han was in danger of extinction from the intrigues of usurpers, the three met by chance in a peach orchard belonging to Chōhi, and made a compact under oath that they would organise forces and fight together to restore the kingdom to its former glory. Ryūbi, the leader, first allied himself with a certain Sōsō (Ts'ao Ts'ao) but being ambitious for power quarrelled with him and fought against him in a number of inconclusive battles. In one of these, Ryūbi was defeated; his two wives together with his fellow general Kwanyu were captured. That night, one sleeping apartment was allotted to the three prisoners in the hope that temptation might lead to an incident likely to split the friendship of the two allies. But Kwanyu was faithful to his old comrade, refusing to enter the room and spending the whole night with lantern and sword in hand guarding the entrance. Kwanyu died in battle in the year A.D. 219.

In the following year Ryūbi was able to found the dynasty of Minor Han and proclaim himself Emperor of China. At one time when entertained by a local ruler, the castle was besieged during a feast and there seemed no way of escape. The only place not surrounded was a steep battlement, at the foot of which ran a ravine with a rushing stream. The Emperor mounted his horse, made for the battlement and escaped by clearing the torrent with a leap of over thirty feet. The third Hero of Later Han was famous for many exploits, not least being 'The Episode of the Undefended City'. Hearing of the approach of an enemy in overwhelming numbers, and his allies having failed to arrive, he ordered the evacuation of the city with the exception of one or two old men, one of whom was set to sweep the road. He, himself, sat in a room over the gate playing the harp. The enemy came and were soon enjoying themselves looting and drinking. Chōhi was able to send word to his army which had by this time been joined by the allies. They now returned in force and by making a surprise attack on the unwary looters were able to achieve a notable victory.

SHOKATSU-RYŌ, better known by his literary name KŌMEI, was a military tactician, eight feet in height, who gave valuable advice to Ryūbi in the wars which led to the establishment of the Later Han dynasty in the 3rd Century A.D. He began life as a hermit, poring over his books, until Ryūbi, after much effort, persuaded him to become one of his generals. In this capacity he waged war against rival kingdoms and rebel tribes.

On one occasion he sent the court headdress of a lady as a mocking suggestion of timidity to a cautious and hesitating opponent, who was thus provoked to do battle.

When fifty-three years of age he had a premonition that his life was drawing to a close and resorted to magic to ward off the dread spectre of death, but the exciting news of a victory was too much for him and he died of the shock. Before he expired, however, he devised a trick whereby he could serve his master even in death. He gave orders that in an approaching engagement his body should be placed on the battlefield with two pigeons sewn in his sleeves. A group of the enemy, startled by the movement of what they were sure was a dead body fled from the spot and caused a panic which gave time for reinforcements to arrive and save the day.

ROSEI, said to have lived in the 7th Century A.D., is noted for his famous dream. Discontented with the dreary life in his native Chinese village, he went forth to seek his fortune. While awaiting his simple repast of millet at an inn, he happened to rest his head on a magic pillow when lo! he dreamed that he had risen to be a minister of state, yea more, that he had married the Emperor's daughter; indeed he dreamt that he himself had become Emperor, when he was awakened by a maid saying his millet was ready. He took comfort in the thought that life is but an empty dream and so returned home, with no more feelings of discontent.

RITAIHAKU. A celebrated poet of China, A.D. 699-762. His association with the Court was not happy and he spent most of his life wandering about the country enjoying the beauties of nature and the pleasures of wine. He was one of the 'Immortals of the Wine Cup'.

SHŌKI, the *Demon Queller* [Pl. 17, 1]. Shōki was alleged to be the ghostly protector of the Chinese Emperor Ming Hwan (Jap. Meikō), who lived in the 8th Century A.D. This Emperor, while ill, had a dream in which he saw a demon in the act of stealing the flute of his mistress, when a stalwart ghost appeared and overcame the robber. In reply to his Majesty's question as to whom he was indebted for this deliverance, the ghost replied that he was Shōki, the Demon Queller. He went on to relate how, when in the flesh, he had been a student, who, failing to pass the state examination, had committed suicide. Overcome with gratitude by the magnificent funeral accorded him by the Emperor of the day, he determined that he would show his appreciation of this honour by devoting his ghostly energies to driving out the devils that infested the country. However successful he may have been in his own land, Shōki seems to have had a hard time when he transferred his activities to Japan. Success came seldom and failure often, for the netsuke carvers generally portray him as a majestic figure in martial attire, outwitted by the mischievous little demons. They capture the frightened Queller under his own hat or elude his blows by clever dodging.

YŌKIHI (Chinese: Yang Kwei-fei) [Pl. 8, 4]. The beauty and charm of this fair lady, the daughter of a petty official, so attracted the Emperor Meikō (Chinese: Ming Hwang), A.D. 713, that he had her as his chief concubine. Hitherto this Emperor, also known as Genso (Chinese: Hsuan Tzung), had been a wise ruler but so enamoured was he that he gave himself up to frivolity and neglected the affairs of state. He is generally depicted teaching the damsel to play the flute. In the end he was compelled to abdicate, while the lovely Yōkihi was murdered.

KEN-EN-SHŪ (Chinese: Hsien-yuan-chi). This famous miracle worker, shown throwing money, lived in the 9th Century A.D. and always appeared young though he was in fact centuries old. He possessed the power of ubiquity. When in search of herbs for his magic potions, he was followed by wild beasts who looked upon him as their protector. Once he transformed into an old and wrinkled hag a court lady who had the audacity to mock at him, but when she begged forgiveness he changed her back into a lovely young girl of sixteen.

Another day, the Emperor gave him a bag full of money which he began to throw to the people outside the gate, the supply being apparently inexhaustible.

RINNASEI. A Chinese poet of the 11th Century who, not wishing his poems to be handed down to posterity, never committed them to writing. He is depicted with a plum tree and one or two cranes.

TŌBA or SŌSHI was a celebrated Chinese statesman, caligraphist and poet, A.D. 1036-1101. Accused of political intrigue he was sent into exile. He is depicted riding a mule and wearing a very large hat.

SHIBA ONKŌ (Chinese: Sze-ma Kwang), A.D. 1019-1086 [Pl. 8, 5]. This famous statesman gave promise of his intelligence and power of initiative in his childhood, proved, it is said, by the following incident. In company with some other boys he was playing with a large jar full of water, when one of them fell in and would have been drowned, had not Onkō grabbed a stone and smashed a hole in the jar. His friend came out with the water.

SHŌHAKU (A.D. 1443-1527). A priest who being a great lover of flowers took the name Botankwa 'Peony Flower'. He was a poet and a great student of literature.

YOJŌ (Chinese: Yu Jang) [Pl. 7, 6]. Yojō is generally depicted cutting a cloak with a sword, not as might be supposed the action of a Chinese St. Martin, but a strange expression of frustrated vengeance. The prince under whom he had served was murdered by a rival named Cho Bujutsu and Yojō swore he would kill the murderer. His first attempt failed and Cho forgave him. Still thirsting for vengeance, he disguised himself as a beggar and hid under a bridge over which his enemy was to pass. Owing to the intervention of a retainer, he was again unsuccessful, and once more Cho, recognising the natural motive of revenge, forgave him. Yojō was overcome by this generosity, and begged for the prince's mantle which he proceeded to slash to pieces. Then, crying that he could not live under the same heaven as his lord's murderer, he committed suicide.

ŌGISHI (Chinese: Wang Hi-che) [Pl. 7, 5]. He was a famous calligraphist reputed to be the inventor of the ordinary square style of writing known as *kaisho*. His son who was also a fine calligraphist is usually shown holding his father's ink stone.

3. THE TWENTY-FOUR PARAGONS OF FILIAL PIETY

Under the influence of Chinese ethics filial piety has for many centuries been a virtue held in highest regard in Japan. As truth may be imparted by hyperbole, so these stories of exaggerated solicitude for parents doubtless helped in the training of the young in the way they should go, absurd as they may seem to the Western mind. At any rate the subjects were popular in the art of both China and Japan.

1. TAISHUN (Chinese: Ta Shun). His filial devotion was maintained in the face of untold cruelty at the hands of his father, stepmother and half-brother. Some compensation came when elephants ploughed his fields with their tusks and the birds did his weeding. His chief reward, however, was when he was twenty

years of age, the Emperor, hearing of his virtue, gave him two princesses as wives and a pre-eminent place in the Government.

2. SŌSAN (Chinese: Tsen Shen). While gathering brushwood, he felt a sudden pain in his throat. He rushed home to find that his mother, wanting his help, had in vexation bitten her finger, an early instance of telepathy.

3. BUNTEI (Chinese: Wen Ti). He was the third son of Ryūhō, the founder of the Han dynasty, 206 B.C. In spite of official duties, he remained for three years at the bedside of his sick mother, never changing his clothes and always first tasting her medicine.

4. BINSON (Chinese: Min Sun). On the discovery how cruelly the boy had been treated by his stepmother, his father decided to divorce her, and only desisted on the son's pleading, 'It is better that one son should suffer cold, than that three children should be left motherless.'

5. CHŪYU (Chinese: Chung Yao). A celebrated disciple of Confucius, who throughout a long life devoted himself assiduously to making his parents happy.

6. TŌEI (Chinese: Tung Yung). He sold himself as a bond servant in order to pay for his father's funeral expenses.

7. ENSHI (Chinese: Yen Tsze). In order to procure deer's milk, the only remedy for a disease of the eyes from which his mother suffered, Enshi disguised himself in the hide of a deer and mingled with the herd. Unfortunately some hunters mistook him for a real deer and were about to kill him. They desisted, however, when they heard his story. He is represented with the antlers of a deer.

8. KŌHAKU (Chinese: Kiang Keh), A.D. 490. He rescued his mother from a band of brigands.

9. RIKUBEKI (Chinese: Luh Su), A.D. 65. While attending a children's party at the age of six, he was given oranges to eat. Two of these he hid in his clothes to take home to his mother, but unfortunately as he was leaving they fell on the floor. His host accused him of greed. Hearing, however, of the boy's intention, he apologised and praised him for his filial piety.

10. SAISHI. Saishi showed her love for her mother-in-law by feeding her from her own breasts for several years when the old lady had become toothless and unable to eat solid food. Apparently this diet so prolonged the latter's life that she out-lived her daughter-in-law, and was able to express her gratitude by calling together all her neighbours and friends to tell them what Saishi had done.

11. GŌMŌ (Chinese: Wu Meng). At the age of eight, when sleeping in the same room as his parents, he assisted their slumbers by allowing himself to be bitten by mosquitoes without brushing them off.

12. ŌSHŌ (Chinese: Wang Siang). In mid-winter when his stepmother expressed a desire for fresh fish, he lay on the ice until the heat of his body caused it to melt, thus enabling him to catch a couple of carp.

13. KAKKYO [Pl. 8, 6]. Kakkyo was rewarded for his virtue by finding a pot of gold. Living in abject poverty, he found it quite impossible to support not only his wife and children, but an aged mother as well. As it would be possible later to have another child but never another mother, he determined to make ends meet by killing his youngest and, greatly sorrowing, set out to dig the baby's grave. To his surprise and joy what should he find in the pit but a pot of gold with an inscription, 'A gift from heaven; let none deprive him of it.'

14. YŌKŌ (Chinese: Yang Hsiang). He saved his father's life and lost his own, by throwing himself in front of a tiger, which unexpectedly sprang from a bamboo grove.

15. SHUJISHŌ (Chinese: Chu Show-ch'ang). When he was a child of seven his mother was divorced and disappeared. For fifty years he searched for her until he found her and took her under his care.

16. YUKINRŌ (Chinese: Yu Kien-low), A.D. 479–510. A sudden pain at his heart called him to his father's deathbed, where he endured a nauseating ordeal in a vain attempt to save his life.

17. RŌRAISHI (Chinese: Lao Lai-tsze). His parents were still alive when he was seventy and in order to save them from any feeling that they might be growing old, he used to dress and play before them in the guise of a child.

18. SAIJUN (Chinese: Ts-ai Shun). In the days of famine *c.* A.D. 8 the only food he could find was wild berries. The sweet ones he took to his mother, keeping the sour ones for himself.

19. KŌKŌ (Chinese: Hwang Hiang). When at the age of seven his mother died, he devoted himself to the care of his father, in summer fanning him all through the hot nights and in winter warming his couch at bedtime with his own body.

20. KYŌSHI (Chinese: Kiang She) and his wife CHŌSHI (Chinese: Chang She). The husband's mother liked to drink the water of a distant river and eat fish from the same place. Daily the devoted pair made a long and troublesome journey to gratify her wish. The gods had pity on them and brought a stream of similar water near their abode.

21. ŌSUI (Chinese: Wang Ngai). His mother was terrified of thunderstorms. After her death, whenever there was a thunderstorm, Ōsui would visit her grave and say, 'Fear not mother, your son is near.'

22. TEIRAN (Chinese: Ting Lan). On the death of his mother, Teiran had made a wooden image of her and to this he daily paid respect. Once when he was away from home, a neighbour called, and because the effigy failed to satisfy him in an act of divination he struck it. On his return Teiran noticed a displeased expression on the face of the statue and learning what had happened went out and gave the neighbour a good trouncing. For this he was arrested but when the full story became known he was elevated to high office in the State.

23. MŌSŌ (Chinese: Meng Tsung) or KŌBU [Pl. 8, 7]. Mōsō was an official devoted to his mother. She became ill and expressed a craving for bamboo soup; nothing else would do. Poor Mōsō was distracted, because it was winter and no bamboo shoots had as yet appeared. However, he went to a bamboo grove, and supporting himself by embracing some of the last year's growth began weeping copiously. Looking down, he saw with surprise and joy that his warm tears had melted the snow and peeping through the ground were some fresh shoots. These he took home and the soup they made not only satisfied his mother's craving but restored her to health.

24. KŌTEIKEN (Chinese: Hwang Ting-kien), A.D. 1045-1105. He was a celebrated poet and official who, in spite of his lofty social rank, expressed his devotion towards his mother by performing on her behalf menial household services.

3

Japanese Legends and History

STORIES FROM HISTORY

The following stories have been selected as those most frequently illustrated in netsuke. They are not intended to be a summary of Japanese history, nor are they necessarily the most important episodes, though some of them are of special interest and significance. Many are legendary.

JINGŌ* KŌGŌ (The Empress Jingō) is remembered for the part she played in the conquest of Korea about A.D. 200. When her husband, the Emperor Chūai, died she concealed his death and assumed command of the expedition, undeterred by the fact that she was pregnant at the time. The birth of her child was miraculously delayed until her return to Japan three years later. She retained the regency until her death when her son Ojin Tennō was seventy. He reigned for forty years and after his death was worshipped as Hachiman, the God of War, although there is no record of any military activities on his part beyond being carried in his mother's womb during the victorious expedition to Korea. Both mother and son were much assisted by the wise counsels of Take-no-uchi no Sukune, famed as a Japanese Methuselah as he lived to the age of two hundred and eighty, or some say three hundred and sixty years.

YAMATO-TAKE is the title meaning 'Bravest in Yamato (i.e. Japan)' by which O-usu, one of the many sons of the twelfth Emperor Keiko (A.D. 70-130), is best known. O-usu's strength and violent nature were revealed when as a boy he slew his brother by tearing him limb from limb. Alarmed by such behaviour in his son, the Emperor thought it expedient to find an outlet for his exuberant ferocity by sending him on an adventurous expedition to subdue a revolt among the aborigines of Kyushu. Young O-usu, as he approached the camp of the rebel chieftain, thought guile as important as strength, and assuming the guise of a dancing girl managed to obtain entry to the place where the chief with some of his followers was feasting. Infatuated with the beauty of the visitor, the chief invited the 'damsel' to sit beside him. When the company were bemused with drink O-usu suddenly drew his sword and set upon his host who, as he was dying, bestowed upon his slayer the title of *Yamato-take*, 'the Bravest in Japan'. The remainder of the company fled but were soon overcome by O-usu's retainers.

Some time later, Yamato-take was sent to subdue the savages of the Eastern Regions. They sought to drive him back by setting on fire the reeds of the plain. The young warrior was wearing the famous sword which the deity Susano-o had found in the dragon's tail (p. 51). This he drew and slashing about cleared a space which effectively stopped the oncoming flames. Then, taking a tinder box which hung from his girdle, he started a new fire which soon spread until it had surrounded and destroyed the wicked barbarians.

PLATE 9: JAPANESE LEGENDS AND HISTORY
1. Ono no Komachi.   *V & A*
2. Kintoki. H. 1½″.
3. Expedition against Shūten Dōji. H. 1¼″.
     B.M.
4. Arm of Oni. Watanabe Tsuna story.
     L. 2″.   *V & A*
5. Tamamo no Mae and the nine-tailed fox.
H. 1¼″.   *V & A*
6. Yasumasa and Kidomaro.

* or Jingu.

KAMATARI (NAKATOMI NO), A.D. 614–669, was the founder of the powerful Fujiwara Clan which for many generations supplied Chief Ministers of State and throughout Japanese history has had the honour of providing wives and concubines for the Emperor. He rose to power by exposing the disloyal intrigues of the rival Soga family and is famous for introducing the revolutionary political and judicial changes known as the Reform of Taika (A.D. 645). Great statesman though he was, it is strange that he should popularly be remembered for the legends that have gathered about his name. Here is one of them, about a very precious jewel which came into the possession of Kamatari's daughter in China whither she had gone to marry the Emperor. She decided to send it to her native land to enrich a temple specially built for it, and entrusted the carrying of it to a trust-worthy retainer named Nanko. Somehow, Ryujin, the Dragon King of the Sea, got wind of the enterprise, and determined to capture it and for this purpose sent a host of devils to intercept Nanko's ship. In this they failed for Nanko and his followers fought bravely and drove off the demons. Direct attack being unsuccessful, trickery was tried. As the ship approached Japan a large tree trunk was seen floating on the sea, and the sailors, curious about its appearance, drew it on board. To their surprise they found hidden inside a cavity in the trunk a beautiful lady. She managed to charm Nanko so much that he showed her his treasures including the precious jewel, which the siren grabbed, and jumping overboard, swam off before they could stop her. She took her spoil to the palace of the Dragon King. When Kamatari heard the news he was so distressed that, over-come with grief, he retired from the world to the wilds to live a hermit's life. However, he had some consolation in meeting a lovely fisher girl who ministered to his needs and lived with him as his wife. When a son was born, Kamatari told her his past history. This filled her with sorrow as she felt quite unworthy to be the wife of a nobleman, and she made up her mind to commit suicide but before doing so determined to make an effort to secure for her lord the precious gem. Diving into the sea, she swam for many miles until at length she reached the Sea King's palace, where by skill and stealth she managed to find and capture the jewel. With this she escaped, hotly pursued, and when attacked drew a knife and plunged it into her bosom, causing her streaming blood to form a veil which hid her from her pursuers. Rising to the surface she was dragged aboard Kamatari's boat in a dying condition. Within the gash in her bosom, her lover noticed something glittering and there, to his astonishment, he found the famous gem, won for him by the devotion and courage

of the fisher maiden. The jewel was taken to the Shrine pre-pared for it and placed as an attribute in the hand of a statue of Buddha, a worthy symbol of self-sacrifice.

ROKKASEN, the six famous poets of the 9th Century A.D., were Ariwara no Narihira, Sōjō Henjō, Kisen Hōshi, Ōtomo Kuro-nushi, Bunya no Yasuhide and Ono no Komachi.

NARIHIRA (ARIWARA NO), A.D. 825–880. Narihira, a handsome nobleman of high rank, was one of the Rokkasen, the six famous poets of the 9th Century. His diaries are reputed, though without proof, to be the source of the amorous adventures of the Ise Monogatari, written in the following century. One of these is undoubtedly historical. He had a love affair with a young lady of the Fujiwara family. Her father broke up the union, making her marry the Emperor Seiwa, whereupon Narihira became a monk. Usually, however, he is depicted as a courtier wearing a headdress known as a Oikake Kammuri, with ear pieces like fans, and viewing the beauty of natural scenery [Pl. 40, 3].

KUZUNOHA [Pl. 11, 2]. According to a strange legend this lady was the fox wife of Abe no Yasuna who died about A.D. 931. Wandering near a fox shrine (Inari) one day, Yasuna saw a fox pursued by hunters. He managed to catch the frightened creature and hide it under his coat until an opportunity offered to let it escape. Several months later, he married a beautiful girl by whom he had a son, the famous astronomer Seimei (A.D. 920–1005). After three happy years his wife died or left him (the legend varies) leaving a message that she was the fox he had saved at the Inari Shrine.

ONO NO KOMACHI [Pl. 9, 1]. In youth a dazzling beauty with a mind 'illumined by poetic fire and sparkling wit', and in old age ugly, enfeebled, clad in unclean rags, sitting by the wayside begging, her life is a notable commentary on the Buddhist text 'All is vanity'. Her story is mostly legendary, the time and place of her birth as well as that of her burial being shrouded in mystery. She was supposed to have lived in the 9th Century, the daughter of a man of noble rank, a brilliant ornament in the highly culti-vated circles of the Imperial Court. She excelled as a poet, counted as one of the six most famous poets in Japanese history, and many verses attributed to her are included in the great anthology Kōkinshu. On one occasion, she was charged with cribbing a poem from an old collection, a copy of which was

Negoro Lacquer. Simple netsuke of a boy in the mouth of a sack, a type which could have been used by the lower classes, signed Toku.

Negoro Lacquer, Shishi on a rectangular base, a subject often found. Many have seals cut into the bases.

Aesthetic and botanical subjects are very popular with netsuke carvers. Here both are expressed in a simple cluster of gourds and foliage in smooth white ivory. 18th Century.

Douglas J. K. Wright, London

Left to right: Wood, recumbent water buffalo beautifully carved by Toyomasa and in this instance the artist has used natural horn for the horns.

Ivory figure of a seated monkey with a chestnut finely carved and signed by Masatami, an artist who specialised in monkey subjects.

Douglas J. K. Wright

Ivory, Shoki astride a crouching Shishi. Shoki fierce-looking and holding a drawn sword. Signed Masatoshi, a good example of 19th century netsuke and representative of the subjects used during this period.

Recumbent Shishi, again a typical example of subject matter and with the added decoration of semi-precious stones such as coral. Here the ball has the decoration. Signed Yukan.

Douglas J. K. Wright, London

Top row, left to right: Ivory: two minute frogs on a snail shell, signed Ransen. Kagamibuta: Frogs under the moon carrying a lantern. Black lacquer: No dancer in pearl and ivory inlay, signed Shibayama, late 18th century.

Lower row, left to right: Black lacquer box netsuke: cock in red and gold takamakiye. Ivory *manju:* the takaramono (precious things) in pearl lacquer, tortoise shell, etc. signed Shibayama. Shitan wood: gold lacquer carp ascending waterfall.

Dennis Collection

Ivory, one of the most popular subjects, quails and millet. This example by the well-known artist Okatori.

Wood, a most interesting stylised chicken squatting with tail erect, signed Seishu, 18th century.

Douglas J. K. Wright, London

Tonkotsu, tobacco box, with netsuke en suite. Both signed Minko, a netsuke artist famous for his tigers and often copied.

Dennis Collection

Ivory, compact ball-shaped netsuke decorated with chrysanthemums and leaves, the top with pearl butterfly and horn dragonfly, underneath a plum blossom in pearl, silver ring attachment.

Wood. Early netsuke forms were influenced by the simple everyday objects found around and about the countryside, pebbles, pearl and shell fragments along the seashore and fragments of wood, the latter here expressed in a small fragment of driftwood simply lacquered with vine leaves, a wasp and a copper ladybird.

Foreign objects found their way into Japanese netsuke forms and a Chinese crystal ball found itself readily adaptable. A pleasing copper gilt mount styled as Mons of the Doi, Inagaki and Hisamatsu families and complete with a ring for the cord, gives the ball a new life as a compact netsuke.

Douglas J. K. Wright

Netsuke depict many figure subjects from Japanese life and legends. The three here show the variety possible. *Left to right:* Foreigners in Japan represented by a standing figure of an Egg-tester, the figure in wood and the egg itself in ivory and held up to the left eye, a good subject for a collector and not too common. Poetess Ono Komachi as an old hag beautifully carved and stained in ivory, signed Shoraku. Finally an excellent Ghost subject, a female Ghost rising above a standing man leaning back in awe, representing perhaps Hangon Ko.

Left and right: Dennis Collection.
Centre: Douglas J. K. Wright

Recumbent Shishi in ivory on a rectangular base with rounded corners. A typical subject and exceptionally well carved with the added attraction of Shibayama style inlay popular with collectors in the Western World.

Wood, monkey with huge peach. A well represented subject in netsuke and nearly always with expressions and mannerisms true to life, this example is signed with a Tensho seal.

Douglas J. K. Wright

Left to right: Stagshorn beautifully carved as a Kappa, Asakusa school.

Wood, Shishi on an openwork garden stool, this example with strong Chinese influence, 18th century.

Douglas J. K. Wright

Left to right: Walrus ivory mask of an Oni, signed Kinjosai. 19th Century, the Ivory nicely mellowed.

Red Lacquer Mask of a Demon, eyes of glass backed by silk. Circa 1800.

Ivory of good quality, the subject a recumbent water buffalo with a figure of a farmer squatting to tie his shoe. An excellent example by Minkoku and possibly the second artist of this name, both of them were well-known figure carvers.

Ivory, an everyday scene. A traveller resting beside his horse. 19th Century.

Douglas J. K. Wright, London

Ebony mask of Hannya, finely carved and with the eyes well detailed in natural horn of rich brown colour, signed Tomotada. 18th Century. (Note: The Character used for Tomo in this instance being the Eight stroke character page 270 of Koop and Inada).

Douglas J. K. Wright, London

Wood, seal subject, most seals are of Chinese or foreign influence. Here a Tiger with raised paw in the Hakuryu style squats upon the square seal cut base, 18th Century.

Wood, typical Tiger subject, signed in Sosho in the style of Kokei.

Douglas J. K. Wright, London

Left to right: Square solid Manju decorated t simulate painting in a skillful combination katakiri and inlay, the subject a Badger in t guise of a priest in a long robe and before hi a mokugyo. The reverse with two other symbol relating to the subject, namely a hossu and ju sceptre. Signed by an excellent artist DOSHOSAI

Hako or box netsuke in gold fundame lacquer the cover with a bird in flight hovering over wistaria branch, the bird a swallow inlaid Shibayama work with the other details in taka makiye on nashiji ground. 19th Century.

Lower middle: Rare material, Haliotis or white coral simply and effectively carved as a Kiku bloom, centre of chased gilt metal piercing the centre and terminating at the back as the cord attachment, period 1800.

Douglas J. K. Wrigh

The difficulties of the beautiful Amas and their amorous octopus friends are shown by the Japanese in mostly humorous vein, here exceptionally well carved by Masakatsu, an outstanding artist of the 19th Century. A young maiden has difficulty in resisting the advances of the creature, as she pulls away from her cheek a caressing feeler.

Douglas J. K. Wright

Fine ivory figure of Raiden the Thunder Kami kneeling upon a bank of clouds. Raiden, hand held to head, ponders and puzzles on the loss of a drum and how he can reclaim it, in his hand a hank of rope and behind his head the rest of his drums. A well carved netsuke by the master Kaigyokusai.

Douglas J. K. Wright

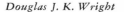

PLATE 10: JAPANESE LEGENDS AND HISTORY

1. Benkei with Miidera bell. H. 1⅝″.   *2.* Yoshitsune at Gojō bridge. H. 1¾″.
     B.M.   B.M.

3. Tadatsune slaying wild boar. H. 1½″.   *4.* Tomoe Gozen and Wada no Yoshimori

5. Soga Gorō.   *6.* Saigyō Hōshi with silver cat. H. 1¾″.

produced to substantiate the accusation. She called for water and washed the page, thereby causing her poem to disappear, thus proving that the ink was new and not part of the original text. In fact, it was the work of a rival who had overheard Komachi reciting the poem and had written it in a blank space of the ancient book.

Another story is that of a lover whom she promised to marry if he would visit her faithfully for one hundred nights. He came regularly for ninety-nine nights but failed to appear on the hundredth, alas! not through any falling off of affection, but because on the journey he had been frozen to death. Some say that the poverty of Komachi's old age was a voluntary penance for the harsh treatment of her lover.

TŌFU (ONO NO), or MICHIKAZE, A.D. 894-964. A celebrated calligraphist. In his youth his writing was poor and he failed several times to gain advancement at Court, until one day, watching a tree frog in a pond making numerous efforts to jump on to an overhanging branch until at length it succeeded, he determined to persevere in his efforts to write better and in the end attained his ambition, becoming a famous writer.

RAIKŌ [Pl. 9, *3*]. Raikō or Minamoto no Yorimitsu was one of the most famous of Japanese heroes, whose exploits are largely if not entirely legendary. His death is said to have been in A.D. 1021. It was a time when the rule of the Fujiwara family was giving way and the authority of the Central Government was beginning to break up, portending the great struggle for unification to be carried out a century later by Yoritomo. The disorder of the day is symbolised in the demons and monsters who were reputed to infest the land. It was in his expeditions to destroy these monsters that Raikō gained immortal fame. He was usually accompanied by his four trusty retainers, Watanabe no Tsuna, Usui no Sadamitsu, Urabe no Suetaka and Sakata no Kintoki. One of these exploits was the slaughter of Shūten Dōji, literally Great Drunkard Boy. This horrible monster lived on human flesh, washed down with prodigious draughts of *sake*. With his gang he lured innocent girls to his lair to satisfy his lust and vicious appetite. The Emperor determined to rid the country of this fearful creature and entrusted Raikō and his brave henchmen with the task. Disguising themselves as Yamabushi, or travelling monks, they set out. Near Shūten Dōji's stronghold, they encountered a young girl washing the bloody garments of a relative, one of the victims. She assisted them by pointing out the way to the fortress. At the gate they were met by an attendant who admitted the monks with mock courtesy, secretly enjoying the prospect of a good meal for his master. Once inside Raikō and his followers began their strategy by entertaining the company with a dance, and assisting in the festivities by passing round quantities of *sake* they had secretly drugged. Before long, the Drunkard Boy and his companions were overcome with stupor. Seizing their opportunity the monks threw off their disguise, drew their swords and dispatched Shūten Dōji and all his wicked retainers. With great joy Raikō and his faithful four, returned to Kyoto, the capital, accompanied by the ladies they had delivered, and laid at the feet of a grateful Emperor the head of the ogre.

Raikō had another great adventure in the destruction of the Tsuchi Gumo or Earth Spider. It happened in this way. Travelling one day with his four companions, he observed a strange fiery cloud in the sky, which assumed the form of a skull. Following this cloud they were led to a ruined castle on a hill not far from Kyoto at the entrance of which was a female of uncanny and indeed horrible appearance, accompanied by a band of goblins. Forcing their way past this gang, they beheld a dazzlingly beautiful woman and at that moment found themselves entangled in warm green cobwebs. Raikō made a thrust at the apparition with his sword which, to his astonishment, broke in his hands and was covered with strange white blood. More of this curious liquid was spattered on the ground at his feet and beyond, forming a trail which led into a gloomy cave. Following this trail of white blood through labyrinthian passages, they came on an enormous spider with a head twenty-five feet long, covered with hair like cotton fibre. It was groaning with pain, the cause of which was evident for in the midst of its body was the point of Raikō's sword. Undaunted, Raikō and his companions rushed on the monster, cutting right and left the cobwebs which enveloped them. The beast was killed at last and from the wound in its body there poured out skulls of one thousand nine hundred and ninety victims of the Earth Spider's cruel activities.

The dance of the Earth Spider was performed by the Kabuki Dancers when they visited London in 1955.

WATANABE NO TSUNA. Watanabe not only associated with Raikō in his adventures, but was also the hero of great and strange exploits of his own. Chief among these was an encounter with a demon at the gate of Kyoto called Rashōmon. This happened in the days of the Emperor Enyū in the latter part of the 10th

Century, an age of trouble and disorder when people were frequently attacked in the streets and carried off, no one knew where. There was a widespread belief that the cause of these disappearances was not the work of bandits, who were indeed plentiful and active, but was due to the activities of supernatural demons. One of these was said to haunt the gate of Rashōmon, every night attacking travellers, but no one had had the courage to fight it. Tsuna was commissioned by the Emperor to undertake this hazardous task. So to the gate he went and sat on guard all through the night expecting an attack, which did not come. Towards morning, however, when he had become somewhat drowsy, he was startled by feeling his helmet grabbed from above. In a flash, he drew his sword and swung it over his head. A huge arm [Pl. 9, 4] fell at his feet and a horrible creature went off into the darkness shrieking. Picking up the dismembered arm, he found it to be undoubtedly that of a demon, for instead of hairs it was covered with quills, and at its finger tips there were claws. Tsuna carried his trophy home and put it in a strong box. Not long after, he was visited by an old woman, who said she had nursed him as a child and therefore took great pride in his brave adventures of which she had heard much. She got him talking of these and after much wheedling persuaded him to show her his latest trophy. No sooner was the box opened, than the old woman turned into a demon, grabbed the arm and made off with it.

There is another version of the Demon's Arm Story. Tsuna was sent by his master Raikō with a message to a remote village called Ichijo. Having fulfilled his task, he was returning late at night when as he was crossing a bridge, he met a lovely damsel who asked for his protection on the dangerous road leading to her home. The chivalrous Tsuna put the girl on his horse and trudged along beside her. Suddenly the fair one turned into a dreadful demon and grabbed him by the hair shouting 'My home is on Mount Atago'. He drew his sword and cut off the demon's arm, as she flew away shrieking. Carrying it home, he lost it as in the other tale.

USUI NO SADAMITSU. The second of Raikō's retainers, Sadamitsu, was the son of a cooper, whose wife died, leaving the father with the problem of looking after a prodigiously vigorous child. So strong was he that at the age of two when his father tied him to a heavy millstone, he was able to crawl about dragging the stone after him. The story of his great strength reached the ears of Raikō who sent for him and brought him up as one of his faithful four.

URABE NO SUETAKA. The third of Raikō's retainers. Returning home one dark night, Raikō was met by a ghostly creature who pressed a bundle into his arms and then faded into nothingness. The bundle grew heavier and heavier until, opening it, he found within a large baby boy whom he took home and adopted. He felt sure that the apparition was Ubume, a spectral form of a woman deputed by the tutelary deity of a district to help any woman dying in childbirth by taking the infant and placing him in the arms of the first stranger she met.

SAKATA NO KINTOKI or KINTARŌ, the 'Golden Boy' [Pl. 9, 2], was Raikō's fourth retainer.

The father of this remarkable child was an officer of the Imperial Guard who fell in love with a beautiful girl named Yaegiri, but from whom he was separated because, falling into disgrace, he had to leave the Court and support himself as an itinerant merchant. The girl, after much searching, at length found him but by this time he had become so mentally unbalanced on account of his disgrace that he committed suicide.

She buried her lover and in her grief went to live in a wild and lonely mountain retreat. Here she gave birth to a son, whom she brought up as best she could with no companions but the wild beasts of the forest. As a small child, the boy began to display well-nigh miraculous strength, fighting bears, monkeys and other wild creatures including a giant carp. When he wished to cross a stream he would uproot an enormous tree and use it as a bridge. It happened one day that Raikō, on a hunting expedition, encountered the lad and was much impressed by his great strength. Hearing also the sad tale of his birth, he enlisted the youth as one of his retainers, a decision he never had cause to regret.

KIDOMARU (Hakamadare Yasusuke). Having refused a petty command under Raikō, he became a brigand hiding his identity under the skins of animals. In the end he was slain by the followers of Raikō, who found him hidden in the carcase of a bullock by the roadside.

Once he attempted to kill his brother Hirai Yasumasa [Pl. 9, 6], but the sweet sounds of the latter's flute so charmed him that he desisted.

TAMAMO NO MAE AND THE FOX WITH NINE TAILS [Pl. 9, 5]. There are many stories of foxes with nine tails. One of these concerns Tamamo no Mae, the concubine of Toba Tennō (A.D. 1108–1123). This Emperor fell dangerously ill and the Court Astrologer, Abe no Seimei, diagnosed the source of the trouble as coming from the beautiful concubine, alleging that a halo had been seen around her head in the dark, and that she was really a fox who was bewitching the sick man. To ascertain whether this allegation were true, an altar was erected in the palace and prayers offered for the recovery of the patient. At first Tamamo refused to attend the ceremony but on being pressed, approached the shrine and then suddenly assumed her real shape, that of a white nine-tailed fox, and ran off. She was pursued and killed. She then took the form of the Sessho Ishi or death stone, to touch which, it was said, meant death. Some centuries later a virtuous priest destroyed the stone by exorcism.

YOSHIAKI (Miura no), A.D. 1093–1181. Miura transferred his allegiance from the Taira to the Minamoto side and, though a very old man, waged war together with his son and grandson. In spite of protests from his son he insisted on entering the thick of battle and was shot down by Taira arrows at the age of eighty-eight. Some say he was over a hundred. At any rate, he is reckoned as one of the Sankō or 'Three Old Men', the other two being Urashima and Tōbōsaku (or Take-uchi-no-sukune).

ENDŌ MORITŌ afterwards known as MONGAKU [Pl. 5]. Endō was a skilled archer in the service of the Emperor Sutoku (A.D. 1123–1143). In boyhood he had spent many happy days with his beautiful cousin Kesa, with whom after her marriage to Watanabe Wataru he found himself desperately in love. He sought the help of the girl's mother to overcome the reluctance of his lady love, who indeed was deeply attached to her husband. Failing in this, he informed Kesa that he would kill her mother if she did not accept his advances. Poor Kesa, now in a terrible dilemma at the threat hanging over her mother, or alternately her beloved husband, devised a way out. She met Endō and told him that if he killed her husband she would accept him. She also told him how he could accomplish the murder, the room where the victim would be sleeping, and the wetness of his hair to assist identification. That night after providing her husband with a dainty meal and much wine to induce sleepiness, she put him to bed, but not in the room arranged with Endō. She now put on her husband's clothes, cut her hair and wetted it and lay down in the place she had told Endō her husband would be. The murderer crept in in the dark, felt the wet hair, cut off the head of his rival as he thought, and put it in his sleeve. When he got out into the moonlight and held up the gory trophy, he discovered to his horror it was the head of the woman he loved. Filled with remorse he rushed to the husband, offering his sword and crying, 'Kill me I am not worthy to live.' To this Wataru replied,

'To kill you will not bring back my wife. Trouble me not with thoughts of vengeance, only get out of my sight.' Endō was deeply moved and determined to devote the remainder of his life in the cause of religion. He underwent penance with many austerities and stood for three weeks under the icy waters of the Nachi waterfall. As a monk he was known as Mongaku. In the cause of his faith he was tremendously in earnest, on one occasion even daring to rebuke the retired Emperor for his licentious frivolities. Yoritomo found him useful as an adviser. He is reputed to have died at the age of eighty but the date and place of death are unknown. The story of Endō Moritō is the subject of the film *Jigokumon* (Gate of Hell), shown in London in 1954.

MINAMOTO NO YORITOMO (A.D. 1147-1199). Yoritomo is famous as the victor in the bloody wars which for years raged between the Taira and Minamoto clans. They are known as the wars of Gempei and they arose because the Imperial Government was not strong enough to cope with the rising powers and jealousies of the clans. They came to an end when Yoritomo succeeded in uniting the country under a strong military dictatorship, called the Shogunate or Bakufu, which he operated from Kamakura, three hundred miles from the capital, Kyoto. The Emperor's Court continued as the nominal source of authority but with little or no real power. This dual system of Government under Shogun and Emperor continued more or less in the same form for seven hundred years, that is until the Restoration in 1868.

Yoritomo was the third son of Minamoto no Yoshitomo, a leader in the struggle against Kiyomori, the Chief of the Taira Clan, who had been successful in getting the reins of government pretty much into his own hands. Yoshitomo, however, was defeated by the Taira and afterwards foully murdered. Yoritomo, then a lad of thirteen, had followed his father in this fight, but, unable to keep up with the disastrous retreat, got left behind and fell into the hands of the enemy. Kiyomori wanted to destroy the whole house of Minamoto but was persuaded to spare the young captive at the urgent request of his sister-in-law, who was attracted by the boy, thinking he resembled a son she had lost. Little did she realise that this act of clemency would lead to the destruction of her house. Yoritomo was placed under the care of Itō no Sukechika and Hōjō no Tokimasa. Before long, he seduced the daughter of the former, and ran away with Masako, the daughter of the latter, on the very eve of her wedding to Taira no Kanetaka. The father, Tokimasa, gave chase, but pretended he could not find them for his heart had been won by

the renegade and his mind was reaching the conclusion that the future lay with the Minamoto. So when Yoritomo was called upon to raise the standard against the Taira, Tokimasa accepted Yoritomo as his son-in-law, gave him the support of arms and later became his chief adviser in the establishment of the Shogunate. Both men were helped by the sagacity and strength of character of the lady Masako.

In his first battle at Ishibashi (A.D. 1180) Yoritomo, being greatly outnumbered, suffered a severe defeat, and fled, hotly pursued, to the wilds of the Hakone Mountains. Here he had a hair-breadth escape when he hid in the hollow of a tree, just as his pursuers Kagechika and Kagetoki appeared on the scene. The latter observed the fugitive but pretended he had not seen him and, poking about in the wrong part of the tree, disturbed a couple of wood pigeons, thus proving that Yoritomo could not be there. The reason for this apparently odd behaviour was that Kagetoki, dissatisfied at the way he was being treated by the Taira, was on the point of going over to the Minamoto side, which he shortly afterwards did. This turncoat treachery was not uncommon in those days.

In the early days of the campaign Yoritomo was greatly helped by Kiso no Yoshinaka (p. 38) who raised a force in the north and was ultimately able to get control of Kyoto; but dissention arose between them and Yoritomo's jealousy led to the destruction of his ally. It was this same jealousy which brought about the death of his two half-brothers, Yoshitsune and Noriyori, who by their bravery and skilful generalship had done more than anyone else to help Yoritomo in his triumph over the Taira.

After four years of fierce fighting the Taira were overcome and practically wiped out at the great sea battle of Dan-no-Ura in 1185. As to Yoritomo's character opinions differ. Some say that he was cold, callous, unscrupulous and inordinately jealous and suspicious. His treatment of his half-brother Yoshitsune is cited in proof of this. Others hold the view that there was some cause for his jealousy, and that the fairness and even munificence with which he rewarded those who served him, whether Taira or Minamoto, show that he had a magnanimous heart. Undoubtedly he had great power in imposing his will upon others and outstanding ability in organisation, which enabled him to found the Military Shogunate which set a pattern of government destined to endure for so many centuries.

MINAMOTO NO YOSHITSUNE [Pl. 10, 2]. Yoshitsune was born in 1159, the son of Minamoto no Yoshitomo, by his concubine

Tokiwa Gozen, and was thus a half-brother of Yoritomo. His mother, a Fujiwara and one of the most beautiful women of the day, had attracted the attention of Yoshitomo at an Imperial marriage ceremony. She bore him three sons. After his defeat at Rokuhara, Tokiwa managed to escape with her three children. Few tales in Japanese history are more pathetic than her toilsome flight through the mountains when the snow was stained by her bleeding feet. Her whereabouts was discovered by Kiyomori by torturing her mother, and word was sent that if she did not give herself up her mother would be killed. Such an appeal to filial piety could not be resisted and with an assurance that her mother's life would be spared she returned. She was in her twenty-fifth year and had suffered terrible hardships and yet her dazzling beauty was such that Kiyomori asked her to be his concubine. This she consented to do if he would spare her children's lives, and to this he agreed. Ultimately he grew tired of her and she became the wife of a Fujiwara nobleman. The two elder boys grew up to be priests. It was hoped that Yoshitsune would also take the tonsure and he was placed in the monastery of Kurama-Yama. But Yoshitsune, or to give him his childhood name Ushiwaka (Young Ox), felt no vocation for the religious life. Legend says that at night he used to slip out and study sword-play under the instruction of the Tengu, those mythical creatures who infest the wild woods. At the age of fifteen he made his escape through the good offices of a gold and gem merchant who arranged a plan to get him to the province of Mutsu in the far north. On the journey the caravan was attacked and the 'Young Ox' showed his strength and skill in swordsmanship by cutting off the head of one of the robbers, a giant seven feet in height.

While passing through the village of Yahagi in Mikawa, this lively youth had his first love affair. Put up by the headman, he happened to hear a young lady playing on a *koto*. He answered her tunes by playing the same ones on his flute, with the result that a maid was sent to see who the piper was. Thus he gained entrance to her chamber and for ten days they enjoyed surreptitious love; after which the young man went gaily on his way while the girl, discovering that she was pregnant and fearing exposure, committed suicide. A similar affair occurred in the house of Kiichi Hogan where the youthful Don Juan spent some time studying a famous Chinese book on military strategy, said to have been written in 1100 B.C. (p. 25).

After these amorous adventures the young Yoshitsune devoted himself seriously to martial training and to planning the efforts he hoped to make on behalf of his clan. When an opportunity offered he left Hogan and moved to Yamashima near Kyoto where he would be in a better position to assemble those who might be ready to conspire with him. News reached him of the rising under his half-brother Yoritomo, whose defeat at Ishibashigawa made him all the more anxious to join in the fray. This he did in many battles which lack of space forbids us to describe.

Eventually the Taira were overthrown at the sea battle of Dan-no-ura, and, after a triumphal entry into Kyoto, Yoshitsune proceeded to Kamakura to report to his brother. The latter, however, having become suspicious and jealous, refused to see him in spite of a pathetic appeal for brotherly understanding. Yoritomo ordered his arrest. He returned to Kyoto, where, thinking himself safe under the protection of the retired Emperor, he found relief in sweet dalliance with the beautiful dancer Shizuka. This lady was able to save his life by discovering a plot, and helping him to escape just in the nick of time.

Henceforth he became a hunted fugitive, fleeing from place to place. On all roads the barriers were guarded in the hope of catching him. He had many narrow escapes. In the end, however, he was run to earth by an overwhelming force and realising that escape was hopeless, the unfortunate Yoshitsune, who had done perhaps more than anyone to assist his ungrateful and cruel brother, killed his wife and then himself. On July 27th 1189 his head was laid before Yoritomo. To this day his spirit is worshipped and his memory survives in art and drama as one of Japan's greatest heroes.

BENKEI [Pl. 10, 1]. Perhaps the most popular of military heroes, this trusty follower of the other paragon of soldierly virtues, Yoshitsune, was born about A.D. 1155. Hero worship has embroidered the story of his life so much that it is difficult to distinguish fact from fiction, but legend has served a useful purpose in supplying many subjects for drama and art. With his violent temper and abnormal physical strength he was a problem child, being nicknamed Oniwaka (Young Devil), for whom a strict life in a monastery was thought to be the cure. The remedy was not successful, for the young candidate for the religious life continued his pranks as a 'Young Devil'. On one occasion he carried off on his back the great bell of the monastery of Miidera and brought it to the rival monastery of Hieizan. The bell, however, did not accept this forcible transfer of service, and showed its resentment by refusing to emit a sonorous ring, merely giving repeatedly a faint moan that sounded like 'Take me back to Miidera'. Benkei in disgust threw it down the mountainside, whence it was recovered by the monks of the monastery who owned it.

Later the young Benkei ran away from his religious superiors and, shaving his own head, assumed the guise of a Yamabushi, a free-lance monk, but became in reality a wandering freebooter, a dealer in swords obtained by violence and robbery. On one of these nefarious expeditions he encountered on Gojō bridge Yoshitsune playing his flute and looking more like a young girl than a formidable warrior [Pl. 10, 2]. Benkei demanded the surrender of the youth's sword. Not only did Yoshitsune refuse, but put up a fight with such extraordinary skill and agility that the giant ruffian had to acknowledge himself beaten. He asked his victorious opponent to take him into his service and, when this was granted, showed his appreciation by a life of loyalty and devotion.

An example of Benkei's clever ingenuity and presence of mind occurred when his master Yoshitsune was fleeing from the forces of his vindictive brother Yoritomo. Disguised as wandering priests (*yamabushi*), Yoshitsune with a small band of fifteen followers, including his wife in the garb of a page and the indomitable Benkei, tried to make their way through the mountains to the stronghold of a friend. Several road barriers were passed successfully but suspicions were aroused among the strong guards at the barrier of Ataka. Benkei's early training in a monastery came in useful, as he was able to remove their doubts by producing what he claimed to be a subscription book (*kanjin-chō*) for building a temple, and pretending to read from it authority for their journey. As they were about to proceed suspicion fell on Yoshitsune, but again Benkei rose to the occasion by giving his master a good thrashing for misbehaviour, and thus satisfied the guard that this fellow treated with such indignity could not possibly be the great Yoshitsune.

NITAN NO SHIRŌ TADATSUNE [Pl. 10, 3], was a retainer of Yoritomo, who on a notable occasion saved his master's life. In May 1193 the Great Shogun, wishing to celebrate his victories over the Taira and the firm establishment of his rule in Kamakura, invited a large company of feudal lords to a hunting party on the slopes of Mount Fuji. Suddenly it was noticed that a huge wild boar, maddened by wounds, was rushing through the crowd, making straight for the Shogun and would probably have killed him had not Tadatsune, with great presence of mind and courage, jumped from his horse on to the back of the enraged animal, and, facing backwards, held the beast's tail while he dealt him a mortal blow. As a reward Yoritomo bestowed upon his deliverer a large estate.

When the festivities of the hunting party were over Tadatsune, with a few companions, retired to the gloomy and mysterious recesses of a great cave at the foot of Mount Fuji. Here he held converse with the deity of the mountain, the Buddhist Kwannon.

ATSUMORI (A.D. 1169-1184). As a youth of fifteen Atsumori fought in the disastrous fall of the fortress of Ichi no Tani when many of the Taira made their escape in boats. Riding his horse into the sea, he heard a challenge from the Minamoto general, Kumagai Naozane, who dragged him back to land knocking off his helmet. When Naozane saw what a young lad he was he wished to spare him, but, urged by the taunts of others and the pleading of Atsumori himself to hasten the blow, he cut off his head. Remorse for this led him to become a monk.

ASAHINA SABURŌ was a son of Wada no Yoshimori, a general who supported Yoritomo in the Gempei wars. There is a tradition that his mother was Tomoe Gozen, the amazon consort of Kiso no Yoshinaka, but this is more than doubtful. Most of his life is legendary, except possibly the assistance he gave his father in attacking the mansion of the Regent on May 24th, 1213. Many tales of his Herculean strength are popular, his wrestling feats, particularly neck wrestling (*kubizumō*) with demons, his swimming with a shark under each arm, or twisting iron bars into ropes. Once he astonished Yoritomo at a hunting party by lifting a huge rock and throwing it into the sea. On another occasion when at a drinking bout a squabble arose over a dancing girl's lack of courtesy, Asahina caught hold of the armour of Soga Gorō and tried to drag him into the house. Gorō remained immovable and Asahina tugged so hard that part of the armour broke and he fell over backwards, much to the amusement of those present.

TOMOE GOZEN [Pl. 10, 4]. The lady Tomoe was a very beautiful woman of prodigious strength and undaunted courage, the heroine of many fierce battles. She was the consort of Kiso no Yoshinaka, a Minamoto general who did much to destroy the power of the Taira. Unfortunately, by his arrogance and underhand dealing, he aroused the jealousy and enmity of his cousin and leader Yoritomo, who turned on his ally and sent a large force against him. In the ensuing battle of Awazu (A.D. 1184) Tomoe Gozen took a prominent part. She met the violent attack of Uchida Ieyoshi and slew him. She cut off the head of another. Set upon by Wada no Yoshimori, wielding as a weapon the huge trunk of a pine tree, she wrenched this from his hands and belaboured him with it. She was an amazon indeed! In the end Yoshinaka was killed, but Tomoe managed to escape. Shaving her head, she became a nun and spent the rest of her life praying for the soul of her beloved Yoshinaka.

KAGESUE (Kajiwara Genda). At the battle of the River Uji (A.D. 1184) together with Sasaki Takatsuna he was commissioned by Yoshitsune to lead the way across a ford. There was a race to see who would get across first, but he was tricked by Sasaki, who cried out, 'Your horse's girdle is loose.' Stopping to tighten it, Kagesue was outstripped by his treacherous rival.

SAIGYŌ HŌSHI (A.D. 1118-1190) [Pl. 10, 6] was a palace guard who, when the Emperor retired and became a monk, followed his example. They made pilgrimages together until the Emperor died, after which Saigyō spent his days wandering about beautiful parts of the country writing poetry. In his old age he happened to be near Kamakura where dwelt his old enemy the Shogun Yoritomo. The latter invited him to pay a visit and read some of his poems. He accepted the invitation and, as he was leaving, received from Yoritomo a present of a fine work of art, a silver cat. For such things the poet had no use and once outside the palace gate, he gave it to some urchins by the roadside and went on his way.

KIMI [Pl. 15, 6] was a harlot who lived in the village of Eguchi in the province of Settsu in the 12th Century. The famous poet Saigyō Hōshi on one of his travels was benighted and found shelter under her roof, and in the night had a vision of the Buddhist deity Fugen Bosatsu, who assured him that his hostess, in spite of her disreputable life, was really an incarnation of himself, having gained merit by her diligent study of the sacred scripture. In netsuke she is represented riding an elephant and reading a scroll (cf. p. 53).

MORITSUNA (Sasaki Saburō no). A Minamoto general in the Genji wars. When a Taira army had established themselves in the Fujimoto Castle of Kojima, at the mouth of the River Nishi, they considered themselves safe from attack. Moritsuna, however, elicited the fact that there was a ford from a local fisherman, whom he rewarded by cutting off his head to make sure he would not reveal his secret to the enemy. Then, on horseback, he led

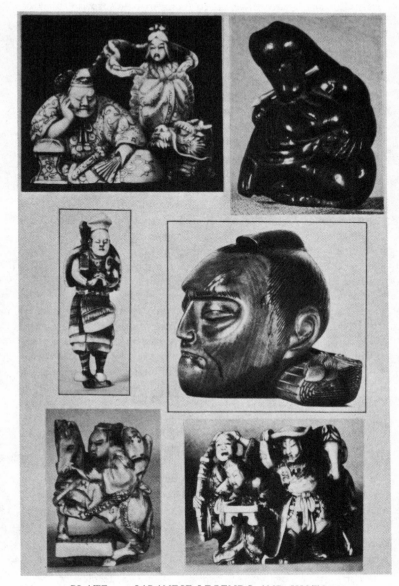

PLATE 11: JAPANESE LEGENDS AND HISTORY
1. Hōjō Tokimasa and Benten. H. 2½″.   2. Kuzunoha. H. 1¼″.
    B.M.
3. Nitta no Yoshisada at prayer. H. 2½″.   4. Severed head of Nitta no Yoshisada.
    B.M.   B.M.
5. Oguri Hangwan.   6. Ōta Dōkwan.

his advance guard across the ford and made a surprise attack on the unsuspecting Taira. Unfortunately, however, there was a delay in bringing up the main body of the Army and most of the Taira managed to escape.

THE SOGA BROTHERS [Pl. 10, 5]. Jūrō Sukenari and Gorō Tokimune were the sons of Kawazu Sukeyasu (cf. Sumō p. 73) who had been murdered by Kudō Suketsune about the year 1177. After the father's death, their mother married a man named Soga and the two boys took that name. From an early age they determined to follow the Confucian adage, 'a man should not live under the same heaven as the murderer of his father', and looked forward to the day of vengeance. The opportunity seemed to have come when Gorō got wind of the appearance of the doomed man at the great hunting party on the slopes of Mount Fuji, which Yoritomo was holding to celebrate his victories. Seizing a horse that was grazing in the field, Gorō vaulted on to its back, and lashing it with a large radish made off post-haste to find his brother and with him accomplish the vendetta. With the help of a courtesan they managed to discover their enemy, tired after the day's hunting and dozing under the influence of drink. Gorō was about to stab him, when Jūrō remonstrated saying, 'To kill a sleeping man is no better than hacking a corpse.' He therefore shouted, 'The Soga brothers are upon you.' Suketsune sprang to his feet and tried to defend himself, but was immediately hewn down. The brothers now fought their way through the followers of their victim in an endeavour to escape. By this time, the alarm had been given and the guards of the Shogun arrived. Jūrō was killed by Nitan no Shiro Tadatsune. Gorō was captured and brought before the Shogun. Yoritomo was at first inclined to spare his life on account of the pluck he had displayed, but in the end felt he could not refuse the punishment demanded by the son of the murdered man. Gorō was accordingly decapitated.

HŌJŌ TOKIMASA (A.D. 1138-1215) [Pl. 11, 1]. Tokimasa was the father of Yoritomo's forceful and able wife, Masako. He took a prominent part in setting up the military Shogunate under Yoritomo. Yoritomo's offspring, being a feeble lot, were unequal to the task of government. This was taken in hand by Tokimasa and his descendants, who ruled under the title of Shikken or Regents, appointing Shoguns who were mere puppets. That the Hōjō rulers, though severe, were efficient and just is generally admitted. Eventually however, weakness and corruption set in and brought about their fall at the hands of the Ashikaga family in 1333.

In early life Hōjō Tokimasa is reputed to have had a remarkable vision of the goddess Benten in the cave on the island of Enoshima. The goddess foretold the prosperity of his house, which would be subject to the condition that he and his family ruled with justice. Should they fail in this, their régime would not last beyond the seventh generation. The divine visitant had the body of a dragon and as she was fading from sight dropped three scales. Tokimasa afterwards produced these as evidence of the reality of the apparition. The three scales became the subject of the Mon or Crest of the Hōjō family.

KUSUNOKI MASASHIGE (A.D. 1294-1336). Unselfish loyalty to the Emperor and calmness of courage were characteristics of one of the greatest heroes in Japanese history. As a youth Masashige showed great diligence in his studies, especially those concerned with the strategy of war, and great physical strength and prowess in the use of the sword. To appreciate the reason for his enduring reputation, he must be viewed against the background of the times in which he lived. The age was a difficult one for the Imperial family, who as descendants of the Sun Goddess were nominally regarded as the source of all authority, but in reality were almost always the tools of subordinate statesmen and powerful militarists. The Shogunate at Kamakura had after the death of Yoritomo fallen under the sway of the Hōjō Regents, who for a time administered the country with great ability, but by the time of Kusunoki had reached a stage of incompetence and corruption that cried aloud for reform. The trouble was hastened by the custom of putting children in positions of authority, while the actual administration was carried on by retired persons or others behind the scenes. The height of folly in this practice was reached when a tutor controlled the Regent, who was supposed to control the Shogun, who was supposed to rule on behalf of the Emperor, who was a child under the control of a corrupt court!

GO-DAIGO, who became Emperor in A.D. 1318, was, contrary to this absurd practice, thirty-one years of age when he ascended the throne. He attempted to put an end to the confusion that prevailed throughout the land, by becoming Emperor in deed as well as in name, and for a short time succeeded. Unfortunately, powerful opposing forces proved too much for him. He was driven into exile and a member of another branch of the Imperial family was put on the throne. For fifty-six years there were two Emperors claiming Imperial authority and a state of disorder and anarchy prevailed. The breach was healed in A.D. 1392.

The supporters of Go Daigo fought hard on his behalf and none with greater courage and energy than the two generals Nitta Yoshisada and Kusunoki Masashige. Nitta destroyed the Hōjō Regent and his followers at Kamakura, but was afterwards killed by the forces of Ashikaga Takauji. It was fighting against Takauji that Masashige also fell. This was in A.D. 1336 at Minatogawa (now part of Kobe), where his strategic advice had been rejected and he was compelled to fight against overwhelming odds. He bade farewell to his son, admonishing him to maintain the soldierly tradition of his family and avenge his death, and then retired to a farm nearby where with one hundred and fifty of his followers he committed suicide.

NITTA YOSHISADA (A.D. 1301-1338) [Pl. 11, 3 and 4]. In the days when the Hōjō Regents were tottering to their fall and the Emperor Go-Daigo was seeking actual instead of merely nominal rule over the country, Yoshisada, originally on the side of the Regent, transferred his allegiance to the supporters of the Emperor. With a force of 20,000 he marched against Kamakura, the seat of government, so strongly defended as to seem impregnable, and guarded by a large fleet of junks in the harbour. Dismounting from his horse he stood on the beach and prayed that the waters might recede to allow his army to pass, ending his prayer by casting his sword into the sea as an offering to the Gods. That night the tide ebbed to such an extent that the war junks were carried far from the shore and Yoshisada with his followers were able to march over the soft sands and attack. Taken by surprise the defenders were completely routed. Takatoki, the Regent, and his principal retainers committed suicide and Kamakura was burnt to the ground. Yoshisada was rewarded with promotion to high office.

OGURI HANGWAN [Pl. 11, 5]. Legend and history are hopelessly mixed in the stories of this adventurous knight, who lived in the early years of the 15th Century. The best-known incident in his life was the taming of a vicious stallion. In flight from the Shogun with whom he had quarrelled and in search of his wife of whom he had been robbed, he sought refuge one night at a large house, which had the appearance of an inn, but turned out to be the headquarters of a notorious bandit called Yokoyama. With designs on their purses, and indeed on their lives, the bandit made a show of giving Oguri and his company a cordial welcome. Now it happened that Yokoyama owned a wild and vicious horse, called from his vile and ungovernable temper Oni-Kage, 'the Demon Chestnut'. If Yokoyama could induce Oguri to mount this beast, he felt sure he would be thrown and killed. He therefore challenged his guest to ride the steed if he could, and Oguri, welcoming the idea of testing his horsemanship of which he was justly proud, accepted the wager. Next morning the trial took place. To the amazement of the onlookers, Oguri managed not only to calm the wild prancings of the animal but to bring him under such control that he rode him to a Go table and caused him to mount and stand with all four feet on this block, thirty inches square. His host could not refuse to pay the wager and after cups of sake Oguri and his companions proceeded on their way, none the worse for their night in the bandit's lair.

ŌTA DŌKWAN [Pl. 11, 6] was the priestly name assumed by the great local chief Ōta no Sukenaga, who was responsible in the 15th Century for building the great castle of Edo, which was later taken over by the Tokugawa Shogun and to-day is the residence of the Emperor in Tokyo. The story regarding Ōta which caught the fancy of artists and netsuke carvers, is that of the clever pun of a country girl he met in a rainstorm. Calling at her house he asked for a straw raincoat called a *mino*. To his surprise she brought him on a fan a branch of Yamabuki (Kerria Japonica). He then recalled a poem 'Although the Yamabuki has several petals, I grieve it has no mino'. Mino means both 'seed' and 'raincoat'.

SHŌHAKU (A.D. 1443-1527). A priest who being a great lover of flowers took the name Botankwa (Peony Flower). He was a poet and a great student of literature.

4

Fairy and Folk Tales

MOMOTARŌ
The Little Peachling
[Pl. 12, *1*]

ONCE UPON A TIME there dwelt by a brook an old woodcutter and his wife, who loved each other and had lived together for many years, happy but for one thing, they had no child. One day the old man having gone to the hills to gather faggots, his wife was doing her washing by a stream, when she noticed a large peach floating by. This she carried home and awaited her husband's return that they might enjoy it together. Imagine their surprise when they cut it open and saw a beautiful baby emerge. They called him Momotarō and brought him up with great care. (Momo means 'a peach' and Tarō is the termination of names of the eldest son.)

When he had grown up to be a strong and brave lad, he said one day to his foster-parents, 'I must leave you for a while, because I am going to the ogre's castle to kill him and bring back the riches he has stored there.' So the old woman made some delicious dumplings for food on his journey and off he went. Before long he fell in with a monkey who asked where he was going. On being told the object of the journey and rewarded with one of the precious dumplings, the monkey decided to join him in the adventure. On they went together and a little further on met a pheasant who also asked what they were up to and hearing the plan also received a dumpling and joined the

adventurers. The same thing happened a little later when they met a dog.

When they reached the ogre's fortress the pheasant flew over the gate, the monkey climbed over the wall while Momotarō with the dog forced open the gate. Together they attacked and overcame the monster. Then, forming a procession, they marched back in triumph, carrying great riches as the spoils of victory. With these Momotarō was able to show his gratitude to his foster-parents and all lived together in happiness, comfort and peace for many years.

THE TONGUE CUT SPARROW
[Pl. 12, *2*]

Once upon a time there was a kind old man who made friends with a sparrow, which he tenderly nurtured. His wife was a cruel and cross old thing, who one day, when the sparrow happened to help himself to her starch, angrily cut out its tongue. When her husband returned from work he found that his pet bird had fled. In grief he wandered through the woods, calling for his dear sparrow, whom by great good fortune he found at last. The sparrow invited him to his home and entertained him right royally with dances and music. When the feast was over two baskets were produced and the host invited his visitor to accept one of these as a little present. The old man modestly chose

PLATE 12: FAIRY AND FOLK TALES

1. The Little Peachling, Momotarō. *B.M.*
2. The Tongue Cut Sparrow. *B.M.*
3. The Magic Kettle.
4. The Tinker with the Magic Kettle.
5. Urashima Tarō riding his Turtle.
6. Urashima Tarō opening his Casket.

the lighter one and took it home. When it was opened it was found to contain gold and silver and other precious things. The greedy old wife was not satisfied and determined to see if she could get more. So out she went to the woods in search of the sparrow. She found his home and flattered him with pretty speeches. He invited her in and provided modest entertainment but said nothing about a parting gift. The old woman, however, was not to be put off and was rude enough actually to ask for a gift. The sparrow then provided two baskets, one heavy and one light, and the old dame, true to her character, chose the heavy one and trudged home staggering under its weight. When she opened it, there sprang out upon her goblins and other horrible monsters, who inflicted on her the punishment she well deserved.

THE CRACKLING MOUNTAIN

Once upon a time there lived an old man and an old woman who kept as a pet a white hare. One day a badger who lived nearby came and stole the food laid out for the hare. The old man caught the wicked beast and tied him up while he went out to work. While the wife was preparing the evening meal the badger flattered her with soft words and at last persuaded her to unloose him. Far from being grateful the horrid animal killed her and made her into soup. Assuming now the form of the old woman, a transformation which Japanese badgers are able to effect, he placed the broth before the hungry old husband when he returned from his work. On expressing his gratitude for a refreshing meal, the badger cried, 'You have eaten your wife,' and reassuming his animal form ran away.

The bereaved man was overcome with grief. The hare came in and was informed of what had happened. 'I shall avenge my mistress's death,' he said, and set off to the mountains to find the badger. He found him carrying a load of faggots on his back. Sneaking up behind, the hare set fire to the faggots. 'What is that curious *kachi-kachi* noise,' said the badger. 'Oh,' said the hare, 'that is the mountain. This is the Crackling Mountain.' So the fire gathered force and badly burnt the badger's back. Even that was less than the criminal deserved, thought the hare, who then applied to the badger's back a poultice of cayenne pepper, causing him to cry out with pain. After many such adventures, the badger, trying to escape, foolishly made a clay boat, which of course melted in the sea, and the villainous old fellow was drowned.

The hare came back to tell his master of all this and the old man and the faithful hare lived together in peace till the end of their days.

HANA-SAKA-JIJI
The man who made dead trees grow
[Pl. 13, 1]

Once upon a time, there lived an honest man and his wife who had as a pet a faithful dog. One day the dog was sniffing in a curious way at a certain spot in the garden and the old people, thinking there must be some food buried which their pet would enjoy, dug a hole. To their surprise and joy they found a pile of gold and silver. With this they were able to live in comfort such as they had never before enjoyed.

Their neighbours, who were covetous and stingy, hearing the story, came and borrowed the dog whom they had hitherto treated roughly and, petting him and feeding him well, led him round their garden. He stopped and sniffed, so with joyful anticipation they began to dig only to find a pile of stinking offal. In their wrath they killed the dog. The owner was stricken with grief and buried his pet with religious ceremonial at the foot of a pine tree. That night, when the good old man was asleep, the dog appeared to him in a dream and told him that if he cut down the pine tree and made a mortar of it he would be suitably rewarded. This the man did and when he began to pound rice in the mortar he found the white grains turned to gold. The greedy neighbours borrowed the mortar, but alas for them the rice did not turn to gold but to filthy rubbish. In their wrath they burned the mortar.

Once again the dog appeared to his master in a dream and told him that if he would sprinkle the ashes of the mortar on dead trees they would revive. So he went to the wicked neighbours saying that although the mortar could not be restored, he would be grateful for some of the ashes as a relic. Sure enough when he sprinkled these on dead trees they began to sprout. So he put them in a basket and travelled about the country helping people by restoring to life dead trees they had valued for their beauty or their fruit.

THE BATTLE OF THE APE AND THE CRAB

Once upon a time a crab, who had picked up a rice dumpling, happened to meet a monkey, who was holding a persimmon seed too hard to eat. 'Would you not like to swop?' said the monkey to the crab, and the latter being a bit of a simpleton

PLATE 13: FAIRY AND FOLK TALES

1. The Man who made dead trees grow. Hana Saka Jiji.
2. The Man with a Wen.
3. Kiyohime.
4. Kaneko.
5. 'Pot-crowned', *nabe kaburi*. H. 2″. V & A
6. Kiyohime dancing in bell. (Surprise Netsuke.)

agreed. They both went home, the monkey chuckling over the way he had diddled the crab. Mr. Crab, however, planted his seed and later on was delighted to see it grow into a tree, but was in rather a quandary as to how he would get the fruit. Just then the monkey appeared and offered to pick it for him. The greedy monkey climbed the tree and enjoyed himself eating the ripe fruit, throwing only sour persimmons to the crab below, who thought it was now his turn to play a trick. So he asked the monkey to come down head first, which he did only to find that the fruit he had gathered fell out of his pockets to be picked up and taken home by the crab. On the way, however, he was waylaid and beaten by the monkey. Just then a friendly egg, a bee and a rice-mortar appeared on the scene and offered to help the unfortunate crab. So they went to the monkey's house, having prepared their plan of revenge. The monkey, little dreaming what was in store for him, came home and lighted the fire to make himself a cup of tea. To his dismay, the egg which had hid itself in the ashes burst with the heat and bespattered the monkey's face. The bee darted out of a cupboard and stung him. As he ran to get away he tripped over a piece of seaweed, and the heavy mortar fell on his head from a shelf above, and made an end of him. Thus he was properly punished for his mischievous tricks.

MAGIC KETTLE
Bumbuku Chagama
[Pl. 12, 4]

The priest of a temple near Tokyo one day preparing to make a cup of tea was in the act of putting the kettle on the fire, when to his astonishment four legs appeared on the bottom of the kettle, the spout turned into an animal's head and a bushy tail appeared. Behold! it was a badger, which began running about the temple. When caught the beast resumed the form of a kettle. The priest felt rather frightened by the presence of such a strange kettle and sold it to a wandering tinker. Before long its new possessor discovered its magic powers, and saw here a good chance of making some money. So he travelled about the country entertaining people with the magic performance of his kettle. It was not long before he had by this means acquired a fortune, and being a religious man brought the kettle back to its original home, made a generous offering to the priest and left the kettle in the temple, where it was kept ever after as a sacred treasure, though never again did it change into a badger.

URASHIMA TARŌ
[Pl. 12, *5* and *6*]

Once upon a time there dwelt in the province of Tango a man named Urashima Tarō. One day, when fishing by the shore of Ejima, he captured a tortoise but, not wishing to cut short the hundred centuries allotted to the sacred animal, he threw it back into the sea. Next morning, happening to pass the same spot, he noticed in a boat tossed by the waves a very beautiful woman, who called to him for help, saying that her companions had perished in a storm and that she alone survived far from her native land.

The kind-hearted Urashima could not resist the appeal of the damsel in distress and promised to escort her to her home, however far away it might be. So he boarded the boat and rowed hard and long until they reached the palace of the Dragon King, where he found to his surprise that the lady he had saved was none other than the daughter of the Regent of the Seas.

So pleased was the grateful Monarch to have his daughter back that he bestowed her in marriage upon her faithful rescuer. For three years Urashima lived with the princess, forgetting all else in the charms of her companionship. At length, however, thoughts of his earthly home came to mind and he longed to see his beloved parents again. His lovely wife was unwilling to let him go, and, weeping, told him that she was the tortoise whose life he had saved. After much persuasion she yielded to his entreaties, giving him as a memento a casket which, she said, he must never open if he wished to see her again. So back he went over the sea to his native land where he hoped to meet his family and friends. On landing, however, all seemed strange and changed and when he enquired about the family of Urashima no one could tell him anything. At last he met a very old man who told him that there was a tradition of a family called Urashima who had lived there many hundred years ago and pointed out the tomb of the last of the line, that of Urashima Tarō, who it was said had perished at sea. Bewildered by this tale and the sight of his own tomb and hoping to find a clue to the mystery, he opened the casket the Sea Princess had given him and lo! from it there issued a pale purple vapour. As it rose in the air, the body of Urashima shrivelled with age and he sank to earth and died an old man who had lived for three hundred years.

In another version of the story Urashima was carried to the Palace of the Dragon King on the back of the tortoise he had saved.

THE MAN WITH THE WEN
[Pl. 13, 2]

Once upon a time a man got lost in the woods and decided to spend the night in a hollow tree. At midnight he was awakened by the sounds of merriment and looking out saw a party of elves dancing. He ventured forth to join them and found to his delight they gave him a hearty welcome. When morning came and it was time to say 'good-bye', they insisted that he should pay them another visit and, to make quite sure that he would, they removed from his head the ugly swelling, the wen that had plagued him for years, saying they would keep it as a pledge. So he went home in high spirits, rejoicing in the loss of his wen.

His good fortune called forth congratulations from friends and neighbours, from all indeed except one who having a wen expressed no pleasure but merely scowled with envy. This fellow, in the hope that the elves might repeat their good deed, sallied forth to the wood and the hollow tree. Sure enough the elves appeared and he danced with them. When the time came for parting, thinking he was the same man who had come before, they brought forth the pledged wen and clapped it on the man's head opposite the one he already had. So home he trudged with two wens instead of one, regretting the envy and churlishness he had shown over his friend's good fortune.

HAGOROMO
The Feather Robe

When Hakuryō, a fisherman, beached his boat on the sands of Mio no Matsubara, he paused as so many others have done at this lovely spot to gaze at Fuji, the peerless mountain, rising above the clouds. Then his eye lighted on a strange and beautiful feather robe hanging on one of the pine trees which line the beach. Stranger still he thought he heard the sound of distant music and sweet perfumes filled the air. Wondering what it might be, he took the robe from the tree and finding it more beautiful than any garment he had ever seen, determined to take it home to his wife. Before he could get back to his boat, however, he heard a voice calling, 'What are you doing with my robe? Please do not take it, for without it I cannot fly back to heaven.' It was the voice of an angel who hovered overhead. Being kind of heart, he could not resist her pleading and restored the robe with which she mounted the sky and disappeared over

Fuji in the sunset. Before leaving, however, she showed her appreciation of his gentlemanly conduct, by performing for him a wonderful dance.

This story is portrayed in the Nō Dance—Hagoromo no Mai, the feather robe dance.

KIYOHIME
[Pl. 13, 3]

In the course of his journeys through the province of Kumano, a priest named Anchin of the Monastery of Dōjōji was in the habit of staying at an inn in Masa-go, whose keeper had a charming little daughter named Kiyohime. Anchin loved to caress and play with this child during his short visits and gave her little presents, never imagining that the affection which the child had for him would one day be transformed into a passion, an unholy passion, which would in the end bring disaster upon them both. But so it happened and when Kiyohime developed into a young woman of great beauty, she began to bestow on Anchin evidences of immodest desire which the priest repulsed resolutely. In vain did the damsel call to her aid the spirits of evil, even to the extent of performing the black magic device of 'the hour of the ox' but such trickery was of no avail for the prayers of the good monk warded off all temptations.

At last, exasperated by her failure, Kiyohime betook herself to the monastery to seek out the man she loved. Anchin, when aware of her approach, sought refuge under the large and famous bell of the monastery whose height was six feet and whose weight was such that a hundred men could not lift it. Kiyohime, whose love had now changed into a furious hate, approached the bell and struck it so violently with a magic striker that the chain which supported it broke and it fell upon and imprisoned the unfortunate monk.

At the same time her beautiful face changed into that of the horrible witch Hannya and her body, becoming covered with scales, was transformed into that of a great serpent encircling the bell with the hot flames of her passion. The monks of the monastery, hearing the row, rushed to the scene, but only in time to hear the faint sounds of their brother's last prayer. When the bell was removed, all that was found were the sad remains of poor Anchin in the form of a little pile of white ashes. As for Kiyohime, she fled never to be heard of again.

There are several versions of the story. One of these is the subject of a Nō dance called Dōjōji, depicted in the netsuke [Pl. 13, 6]. Here the bell is encircled with the dragon but when opened reveals not the unfortunate Anchin as might be expected, but Kiyohime who, reincarnated in the form of a dancing girl, returned to the monastery after many years and entertained the monks with a dance.

KANEKO, or O KANE
[Pl. 13, 4]

A very strong and determined young woman, who, seeing the sacred white horse from a temple running away and knocking over pedestrians in his way, planted one of her clogs (*geta*) upon its halter and stopped it.

NABE KABURI
'Pot-crowned'
[Pl. 13, 5]

At the annual festival of the Temple of Tsukuma in the province of Omi, there is an ancient custom that no woman who has committed adultery shall be allowed to participate in the religious ceremonies unless she carries on her head an iron kettle or pot, and that if she has sinned more than once she must carry pots to the number of her delinquencies. The coy lady in the netsuke required a servant to carry her pots!

O IWA
[Pl. 38, 5]

One great overhanging eyelid covers the protruding eye of this repulsive ghost, while her hands hang like paws ready to pounce on a victim. She is without feet, her lower extremities fading into nothingness, a characteristic of all Japanese ghosts. She had been the wife of a Samurai, Kameya Iemon, who treated her cruelly and in the end murdered her with poison supplied by his paramour O Sode, the daughter of a doctor. Though the lovers were married Kameya had no peace or happiness, being repeatedly haunted by the sight of his dead wife's horrid features which he thought he saw on the faces of people he met. To rid himself of this torment he murdered them one after another. His last victim was his beloved O Sode.

O KIKU or IDO NO BŌKON
The Ghost of the Well

A maidservant, who broke one of ten very precious plates and, though she confessed the accident, was cruelly imprisoned. She escaped and drowned herself in a well. She is depicted emerging from a well counting the plates.

PLATE 14: THE SEVEN GODS OF GOOD LUCK

1. Daikoku. H. 1⅜″. 2. Fukurokuju. H. 1½″. 3. Hotei.
4. Group with Benten in centre playing 5. Group with Bishamon in centre. (Back
biwa. H. 1¼″. *V & A* of No. 4)
6. Jurō or Jurōjin. H. 1⅜″. 7. Ebisu. H. 1½″.

5

Gods, Saints and Demons

THE SEVEN GODS OF GOOD LUCK
(Shichi-fuku-jin)

THESE DEITIES ARE not regarded by the Japanese with any serious religious devotion, probably hardly more than Father Christmas is in the West. Many a child has been soothed to sleep by a nursery rhyme about "Ebis' Sama, Daikok' Sama" and few homes are complete without a picture or image of one or more of these popular bringers of good fortune. They are frequently represented with little regard for their dignity or sanctity in the picture books which were published in large numbers in the 18th and early 19th Centuries.

How or when this heterogeneous collection were classed together, no one knows: the group is certainly not very ancient, though individual members may be. Probably the earliest example of their association is a picture in the British Museum, dating from the end of the 17th Century. Their origin is strangely varied being derived from four sources, Brahmanism, Buddhism, Taoism and Shintoism.

Western writers have attributed to each of them separate functions like the Nine Muses, though strange to say the Japanese themselves do not appear to have troubled about this neat arrangement.

DAIKOKU [Pl. 14, 1, and Pl. 3, 7], with Mallet and Rice Bales, accompanied usually by a rat, is the bringer of worldly prosperity. The name may be read in two different ways according to the Chinese characters used. It may mean 'Great Black' and suggest a connection with the black-faced Buddhist deity formerly placed at the entrance of Indian or Chinese Temples: or it may be written 'Great Country', and refer to Ō Kuni Nushi, the Shinto God worshipped as an agricultural deity, especially in the province of Izumo. The rat who accompanies Daikoku has been looked upon as a warning against carelessness in protecting earthly possessions. Others think that the animal came to be associated with the God because his festival occurs on the Day of the Rat.

EBISU [Pl. 14, 7] is the patron of honest labour, or the provider of daily sustenance for the worker. He is a fisherman with rod and a fish, the *tai*, or sea bream, the chief delicacy at banquets. He is also called Hiruko, the Leech Lord.

He is the one of the seven recognised as having his origin in native mythology and related to Izanami and Izanagi, the progenitors of the race, but as to what exactly that relationship was there are conflicting theories, too complicated to unravel satisfactorily.

He and Daikoku are frequently represented together as Gods of worldly prosperity, and they are sometimes joined by Fukurokuju, the group being known as The Three Gods of Good Fortune.

His festival is on the 20th day of the 10th month, the only deity celebrated during this "month without Gods", when all the other eight millions of the Japanese pantheon are said to

PLATE 15: GODS AND SAINTS

1. Uzume or Okame with mask of Saruta. H. 1⅜″.
3. Daruma. H. 1⅜″.
5. Kwannon. H. 1½″.
2. The Three Wine Tasters: Confucius, Buddha and Laotze.
4. Daruma stretching. H. 3″
6. Kimi as Fugen Bosatsu.

meet at the Great Shrine of Izumo. Ebisu is not with them, not on account of any impoliteness on his part, but simply because, being deaf, he does not hear the summons.

FUKUROKUJU [Pl. 14, *2*]. The name of the old man with the preternaturally tall bald head means good fortune, wealth, longevity. His identity is hopelessly mixed with that of Jurōjin, who often looks so much like him that they are indistinguishable. Some think that he represents Lao-tze (Rōshi). Undoubtedly there is something Taoist about him and it is certain that he hails originally from China. He is accompanied by one or more of the following, the crane, the long-tailed tortoise, a deer, a staff, a manuscript roll and a sacred gem, the first three being emblems of longevity. The lofty bald head makes him an attractive bait for merriment with the netsuke carvers.

JURŌ or JURŌJIN [Pl. 14, *6*] (longlived-old-man) is another Genius of Longevity, but also the patron of scholarly success. He wears the dress of a scholar with perhaps a peculiar head-dress, carries a scroll and perhaps a fan and is generally of solemn mien. Like Fukurokuju, with whom, as has been said, he is often confused, he is usually accompanied by the symbols of longevity, the tortoise and the deer.

BISHAMON [Pl. 14, *5*] wears armour, carries a lance in one hand and a pagoda in the other.

Despite his martial guise, he is not specially associated with military glory, but is regarded as a God of Wealth. A Japanese book says of him that 'he can grant good fortune more swiftly than the flight of an arrow from the bow'. Yet strangely enough he is seldom, if ever, carved as a netsuke apart from the group of seven. As a Buddhist image and in Buddhist picture-books, he appears as one of the Four Heavenly Kings, whose images were among the first subjects to inspire early native sculptors.

BENTEN, short for BENZAITEN (understanding-wealth-divinity) [Pl. 14, *4*, and Pl. 11, *1*]. She is the one lady among the seven, plays a musical instrument, usually a *biwa*, and has for her attendant a snake or a dragon.

Europeans have considered her the deity of matrimonial bliss, but there is nothing in native literature to justify this. One Japanese authority says that she confers upon her worshippers 'wisdom, eloquence, victory in war and money in abundance'.

Unlike most of her companions in the group she is an object

of serious worship, appearing in many forms. Some have identified her with Sarasvati, the Brahmaic Goddess of speech and learning; her image appears with a great variety of insignia in Buddhist temples; she may have on her head a torii, i.e. the gateway of a Shinto shrine.

The Shinto Goddess Itsukushima has been considered a manifestation of Benten or vice versa.

Her shrines are mostly on islands, the most famous being that in a cave on the island of Enoshima, not far from Yokohama. An ancient legend says that, before the island existed, the cave, then under the sea, was the lair of a great dragon who used to devour the children of the neighbourhood. In the 6th Century a violent earthquake occurred and the island arose from the sea. Benten descended from heaven, married the dragon, and thus put an end to his ravages.

HOTEI [Pl. 14, 3], is probably the most popular of the Seven. Excessively fat, exhibiting shamelessly a generous allowance of his great belly, joyously laughing, whether alone or surrounded by hordes of children, he is looked upon as the God of Contentment. He carries a large bag, in which he stores precious gifts, or in which he may envelope himself to sleep or play hide and seek with the youngsters.

Half Taoist, half Buddhist, he is generally understood to have been a Chinese priest of the 10th Century, remembered for his fatness and love of children, with whom he used to play in the streets. It is said that he could sleep in the snow, that he never allowed water to touch his body and that he could infallibly predict the future.

THE TREASURE SHIP OF GOOD FORTUNE

The New Year is the time for welcoming the arrival of this ship called the Takarabune, with its load of wonderful treasures, including the Hat of Invisibility, the Lucky Raincoat to ward off evil influences, the Sacred Key to the Storehouse of the Gods, the Inexhaustible Purse, the Hammer of Chaos, a Feather Robe worn by Buddhist Angels, etc., etc.

The Ship is manned by the gay company of the Seven Gods of Good Luck.

SHINTO

UZUME or OKAME (Pl. 15, 1) is the Goddess of Fun or Folly, with fat cheeks, two spots on her forehead, and a simpering smile. Sometimes she plays with a long-nosed Tengu mask or carries a large mushroom.

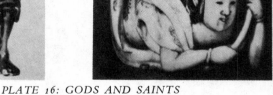

PLATE 16: GODS AND SAINTS

1. Herd Boy, *bokudō*. H. 1¼″.
2. Futen and Raijin or Raiden. Gods of Wind and Thunder. H. 1½″. *V & A*
3. Emma-Ō having a bath. H. 1″. *V & A*
4. Handaka Sonja. H. 1½″. *V & A*
5. Ni-Ō.
6. Buddhist Angel, *Tennin*. L. 2¼″.

Her ancestry is purely Japanese dating from her famous dance before the Sun Goddess in one of the earliest myths about the origin of the race and the Imperial House. The Sun Goddess Amaterasu Ō Mi Kami, or Heavenly Shining Deity, greatly annoyed at the rude behaviour of her brother, Susano-o the Storm God, retired sulkily to a cave, thereby causing the heavens and the earth to be thrown into darkness and gloom. This, of course, reduced the gods to consternation and distress, but happily a clever plan was devised to inveigle the insulted lady from her hiding place. Uzume, a comely Goddess, mounted a tub and performed a dance, which would not be considered quite decent in prudish circles, but which called forth boisterous shouts and laughter on the part of the assembled deities. The curiosity of the Heavenly Shining One was aroused and, peeping from the cave, she beheld a reflection of her own lovely countenance in a mirror, which had been hung with guile for this very purpose. It was too much for her and venturing a step further she was caught and dragged forth. From henceforth the heavens and the earth had light.

Uzume's part in this drama has caused her to be regarded with playful esteem and affection (it could hardly be called veneration!) by merrymakers ever since.

SUSANO-O NO MIKOTO. This deity, known as 'The Impetuous Male', was born from the nose of the Creator God Izanami. How his sister, the Sun Goddess, born from the same deity's left eye, was upset by the outrageous behaviour of her boisterous brother has been related above. Susano-o is said to have descended on the province of Izumo to become the tutelary deity of that part of Japan. Here there once dwelt a terrible eight-headed snake or dragon which terrified the neighbourhood by slaughtering and eating young women who ventured out alone. To the rescue came Susano-o in the form of a warrior. Strategy as well as strength was called for, so the precaution was taken of providing eight jars of strong *sake*, one for each head, to tempt the brute. The bait had the desired effect for the monster had not consumed much before he became drunk, and Susano-o was able to mount his back and kill him. Cutting open the tail, he discovered a remarkable sword which, together with the mirror of the Sun Goddess and the Sacred Jewel, became the Regalia of the Emperors of Japan.

SARUTA HIKO NO MIKOTO [Pl. 15, 1]. A God with a very long nose who blocked the progress of Ninigi no Mikoto (divine grandfather of Jimmu Tennō) as he descended from heaven to

PLATE 17: DEMONS—ONI

1. Shōki, the Demon Queller, catching an Oni.
3. An Oni Triumphant.
5. Bottom of No. 3. Shōki captured.

2. Shōki on the War Path. H. 1¾″. V & A
4. An Oni converted. Buddha removing his horns. H. 1¾″. B.M.
6. Oni impersonating the Gods of Wind and Thunder. B.M.

rule Japan, but who was persuaded to open the way by the charms of Uzume.

Uzume is often depicted fondling a mask of Saruta Hiko, who is identified with Koshin, the God of the roads, and whose festival is celebrated on the 'day of the Monkey'. The three Monkeys (see, hear and speak no evil) are his messengers.

RAIJIN, RAIDEN, or KAMINARI SAMA (Pl. 16, *2*, and Pl. 17, *6*), the God of Thunder (which includes lightning), is a nature deity common to primitive religions. He is represented with a drum, or a circle of drums, usually in a tattered condition. Often accompanying him is FUJIN or FUTEN, the God of the Wind, who is depicted deflating a large bag.

THE THREE GREAT TEACHERS:

SHAKA, the Buddha; KŌSHI, Confucius;
and RŌSHI, Lao-tze

Chinese civilisation was brought to Japan in the 6th Century A.D. by monks of the Buddhist religion which absorbed the primitive Shinto and has remained the chief religion of the country down to the present time. Confucianism was never adopted as a religion in Japan though its ethical teaching has commanded great respect, especially during the Tokugawa period.

Taoism, the religion of Lao-tze, has never been accepted as a religion in Japan though Taoist thought has found a place among some of the Buddhist sects, and Taoist legends appear in the lives of the *Sennin*, and in popular superstitions.

THE THREE WINE-TASTERS [Pl. 15, *2*]. Although all partake of the same wine, one finds it sweet, another bitter and the third sour. Thus, the doctrines of Shaka, Kōshi and Rōshi seem different to the adherents of the three faiths, but in reality all come from the same source.

BUDDHISM

DARUMA [Pl. 15, *3* and *4*, and Pl. 30, *3*] sits with scowling swarthy face, enveloped in his bag-like garments; devoid of legs and sometimes of arms; or standing stretching himself; or being massaged; or in company unsuitable for a saint.

Daruma, as a netsuke, as portrayed in popular art, as a toy, or as a snow man, has fallen far from his lofty position as a Buddhist

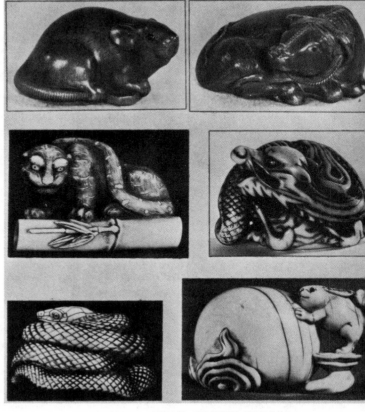

PLATE 18: SIGNS OF THE ZODIAC

1. Rat   *2.* Ox. L. 3″
3. Tiger and Bamboo. H. 1⅜″. *V & A*   *4.* Dragon.
5. Serpent. H. 1½″   *6.* Hare and the Moon. H. 1¼″

saint. The original Daruma or Bodhi Dharma was the founder of the great Zen sect of China and Japan, in which latter country it remains the religion of large numbers of soldiers and intellectuals. He is reputed to have been an Indian prince, who, converted to the Buddhist faith, went as a missionary to China about A.D. 520 and founded the Zen sect.

He began his ministry by sitting for nine years in meditation, neither speaking nor moving, with the result that his legs became paralysed or, as tradition says, withered away. Legend also has it that one day, inadvertently going to sleep, he showed his penitence by plucking off his eyelids and casting them to the earth where they took root and grew as the tea plant, an antidote to sleepiness for holy men. Irreverent artists dispute the continuity of his long meditation, by depicting him stretching himself, thereby revealing legs which show no signs of withering.

The female Daruma humorously suggests the impossibility of a woman remaining still or silent for any length of time, let alone nine years!

EMMA-ō [Pl. 16, 3]. King of the Buddhist Hells, the Judge of the Dead, is usually represented seated, wearing Chinese costume with the cap of a magistrate in front of which is inscribed the character for 'king'. Sometimes he has in his right hand a flat baton, symbol of his office.

His original name was Yama, the Indian King of Hell. In netsuke he is treated humorously with scanty respect.

FUGEN BOSATSU [Pl. 15, 6] is a Bodhisattva, the spiritual son of the celestial Buddha Vairocana (Jap. Dai Nichi Nyorai). This compassionate deity, somewhat feminine in appearance, sits on an elephant and carries a scroll, and bestows upon worshippers the inestimable gift of knowledge.

FUJI HIME, Princess Fuji, the Goddess of Mount Fuji, called 'The Princess who makes blossoms to flower'. She wears a sunhat and carries a twig of wistaria, the character for which, though differing from that of the mountain, is also read *Fuji*. Possibly a Shinto deity.

HERD-BOY (Bokudō or Ushidōji) [Pl. 16, 1]. One of the stages passed through by the Buddhist believer on his journey towards Buddhahood is symbolised by the herd-boy sitting on an ox and playing a flute in sheer joy that he has found the true way.

HANDAKA SONJA (Sanscrit: Panthaka) [Pl. 16, 4]. He was one of the sixteen Arhats or immediate disciples of Buddha, who possessed magical power. He is often represented with a dragon issuing from his begging bowl.

JIZŌ, who holds in his right hand a staff ornamented with rings (*shakujō*) and in his left the Sacred Jewel (*tama*), is the compassionate helper of those in trouble.

He is the patron of travellers, pregnant women and children. His image, frequently seen along the roads, generally has piles of stones heaped about its base. These offerings are said to relieve the toils of children in the other world, who,

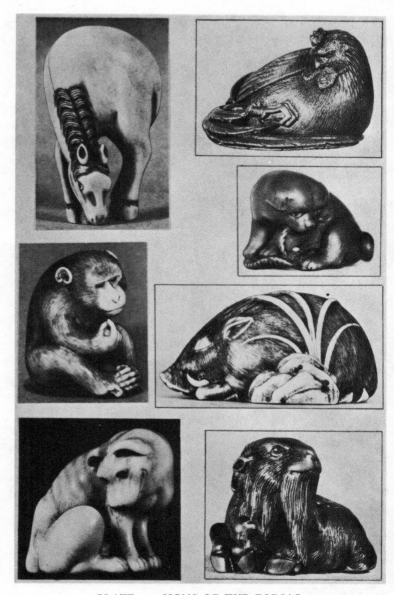

PLATE 19: SIGNS OF THE ZODIAC
1. Horse. H. 2¾″.   *2.* Cock.
3. Monkey.   *4.* Puppy.
    5. Boar. H. 1⅜″.   V & A
6. Dog. H. 1¾″.   *7.* Goat. H. 1¼″.

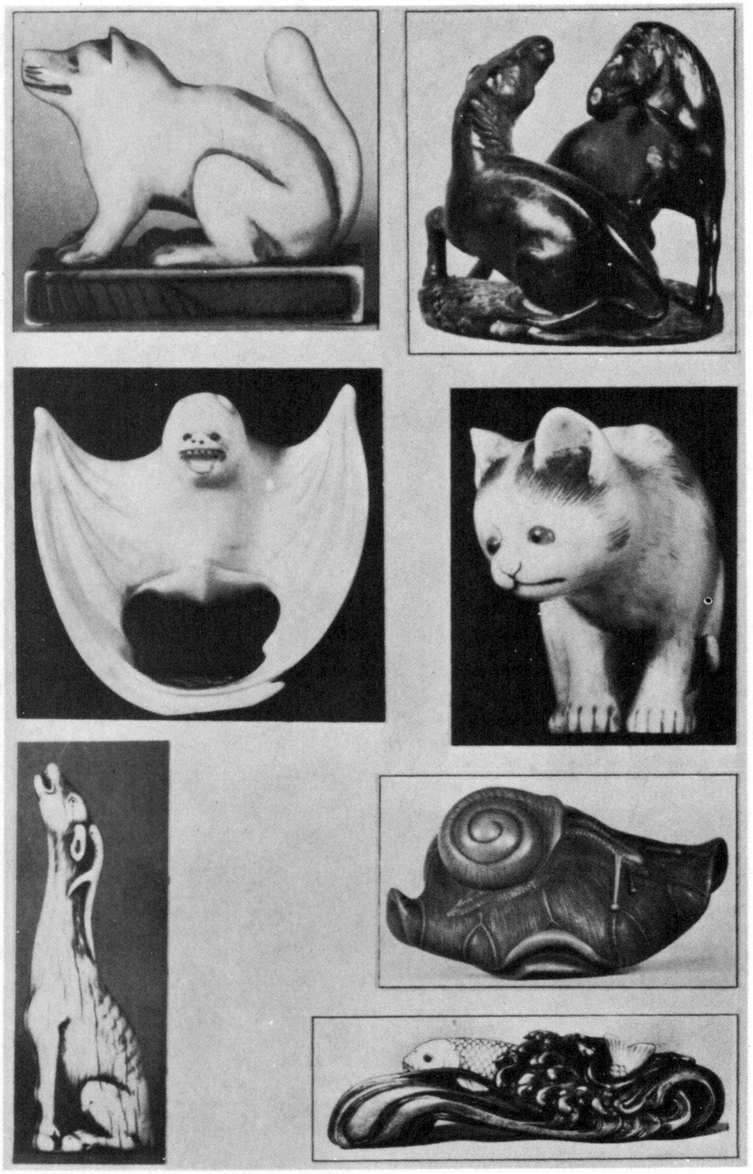

robbed of their clothes by a fierce old hag, are compelled by her to perform a never-ending task of piling stones.

KONGARA DŌJI is one of the attendants of Fudō, the God of Waterfalls, a weird male who carries an iron club. His companion is Seitaka Dōji.

KWANNON [Pl. 15, 5]. This great deity belongs to the class of Bodhisattvas (Bosatsu), that is, beings who have attained all but the highest state of Buddhahood. Being feminine in appearance Kwannon is known as the 'Goddess of Mercy', although Buddhism allows no distinction of sex. The greatness of her compassion may be symbolised by giving her many hands, though this is only one of the forms in which she is depicted. The dragon is one of her attributes.

MONJU BOSATSU, a Buddhisattva. Apotheosis of transcendental wisdom, usually represented seated on a lion and holding a scroll.

NI-Ō [Pl. 16, 5]. The two Deva Kings, Indra and Brahma, who stand at either side of the outer gate of certain Buddhist temples to ward off evil influences. Gigantic in size and fierce in appearance, it is not strange that they should be emblematic of strength and attract the devotion of pilgrims and other pedestrians, who hang before them offerings of straw sandals. Both have little clothing beyond the sacred scarf over their heads. One with open mouth holds a *tokko*, talisman against evil, and the other whose mouth is closed, holds a club. Popularly from their colour they are called the 'Red Demon' and the 'Green Demon'.

RAKAN (Sanscrit: Arhat). A *rakan* is a perfected Buddhist saint. The term is generally restricted to the sixteen apostles of the Buddha Sakya Muni (*Shaka*) or to his five hundred disciples.

SAMBŌ KŌJIN, the God of the kitchen, with three faces and four hands, holding Buddhist emblems. The spiritual God of the Three Treasures.

SANZŌ HŌSHI. A famous Buddhist priest who went to India in A.D. 629 to collect sacred relics and books. After a sojourn of seventeen years he transported six hundred and fifty-seven volumes to China together with many images and other treasures. His companions were a monkey, a boar and a three-eyed demon. His travels are related in Bakin's novel *Saiyūki*.

PLATE 20: ANIMALS

1. Inari Fox. H. 1¼".
3. Bat. H. 1¼".   B.M.
5. Deer.   B.M.

2. Horses. H. 1¼".
4. Cat.   B.M.
6. Snail on leaf.   V & A
7. Carp, *Koi*, swimming upstream.

TANKWA. A Buddhist monk who used to burn images in the hope of finding in the ashes a *shari*, a small piece of gum-like substance supposed to be found in the ashes of a cremated saint. When his abbot remonstrated and pooh-poohed the idea Tankwa said, 'What value is there in an image if it has no *shari*?'

TENNIN, Buddhist angels [Pl. 16, 6]. These beautiful winged maidens wear a robe of feathers and a floating scarf as they fly through the air. They carry the sacred Lotus Flower, or play a musical instrument (cf. Hagoromo, or Feather Robe, p. 46).

TOKKO or DŌKŌ (Sanscrit: Vajra). A bronze ornament representing a thunderbolt, with one or more prongs at each end, used by Buddhist priests as a religious sceptre symbolising the irresistible power of prayer, meditation and incantation, against personal passion, vices and demons. Demons are sometimes depicted playing upon the instrument of their destruction, oblivious of their impending doom.

There are three forms: Dōkō with one prong at each end, Sankō with three prongs and Gokō with five, corresponding to three orders in the Buddhist priesthood, the Dōkō being the lowest.

WAGŌ JIN. The two Merry Genii of Harmony and Concord. One of these Chinese boys holds a lotus, the other a sceptre and a salver filled with gems and corals. They trample on the emblems of good luck.

DEMONS (ONI) [Pl. 17, 3, 4, 5 and 6]. Oni is the generic term for demons or devils. They are usually distinguished by two short horns, claws, sharp teeth and malignant eyes. Occasionally they wear trousers of tiger skin. Oni are attendants upon Emma-Ō, the judge of Hell. The Buddhas may deprive them of their evil powers by removing their horns, and they are sometimes represented with rosaries, or as begging monks, a conversion not taken very seriously. Indeed, the expression *oni no nembutsu*, 'an oni's prayer', is equivalent to 'a wolf in sheep's clothing'. Although their activities may on occasion inspire terror, as in the story of Watanabe no Tsuna (p. 34), they are generally regarded as mischievous imps. Shōki, the Demon Queller (p. 26), is their great enemy who however finds it difficult to control their humorous tricks.

Beans are a potent charm which oni are unable to withstand. At the New Year* there is the ceremony of Oni-Yarai when householders scatter beans shouting, 'Demons out! Good luck in.' In certain temples to-day this custom is observed, usually with much levity, and prominent people, wrestlers, actors, businessmen and even politicians are invited to share the fun.

* Lunar Calendar.

6

Mythical Creatures, Animals and Plants

ANIMALS AND PLANTS

THE JAPANESE LOVE of nature is revealed in the large number of netsuke of animals, insects, fish, shells, flowers, fruit, nuts and roots, carved with realistic skill. The beauty of the thing in itself, its characteristic and life-like pose, its graceful lines or, when in groups, the balanced masses, reveal the sentiments of a nation of artists. Sometimes these objects convey a meaning symbolic of a poetical or legendary allusion, perhaps obvious or in other cases referring to something now inexplicable because the tale or poem has long been forgotten.

Examples of this relation to ancient poetry are found in the association of certain animals and plants so frequent in Chinese and Japanese art, e.g.:

Quail and Millet [Pl. 21, 7]; Peacock and Peony; *Shishi* and Peony;
Tiger and Bamboo [Pl. 18, 3]; Plum Blossom and Moon; *Chidori* and Waves;
Deer and Maple; Boar and Lespedeza; Snake and Tortoise; Crane and Tortoise; Monkey and Peach [Pl. 36, 6].

SIGNS OF THE ZODIAC

Rat, Ox, Tiger, Hare, Dragon, Serpent, Horse,
Goat, Monkey, Cock, Dog, Boar
[Pl. 18 and Pl. 19]

Before the introduction of Western clocks, the time of day was indicated in two ways, one by the Signs of the Zodiac and the other by a numerical enumeration. By the first method, the period from midnight to midnight was divided into twelve hours, the Japanese 'hours' being thus equal to two of our time, and these hours were named after the signs of the Zodiac beginning with the 'Hour of the Rat'.

According to the other method midnight was 9 o'clock and the ensuing hours were denoted by a diminishing sequence 8, 7, 6, 5 and 4. From midday to midnight this was repeated.

European reckoning				Sign of Zodiac			Japanese reckoning
12 midnight	..	..	..	rat ..	..	..	9 o'clock
2 a.m.	..	..	..	ox ..	..	..	8 ,,
4 a.m.	..	..	..	tiger ..	..	..	7 ,,
6 a.m.	..	..	..	hare ..	..	..	6 ,,
8 a.m.	..	..	..	dragon	..	..	5 ,,
10 a.m.	..	..	..	serpent..	..	..	4 ,,
12 mid-day	..	..	..	horse	..	..	9 ,,
2 p.m.	..	..	..	goat ..	..	..	8 ,,
4 p.m.	..	..	..	monkey	..	..	7 ,,
6 p.m.	..	..	..	cock ..	..	..	6 ,,
8 p.m.	..	..	..	dog ..	..	..	5 ,,
10 p.m.	..	..	..	boar ..	..	..	4 ,,

The reason for stopping at 4 was to avoid the confusion that might have arisen when the hours were sounded, three strokes of the bell being always given as a warning. Clocks were made from Dutch models altered to suit the Japanese method of measuring time. The dial was marked with the twelve Zodiac Signs and also with the numerals 9 to 4 repeated twice. There was only one hand which completed the circle once from midnight to midnight, moving anti-clockwise! No wonder Japan has been called topsy-turvydom.

56

The Signs of the Zodiac were used in calendars, not only to mark the passage of time, but also for the important purpose of indicating lucky or unlucky days, months or years. In this reckoning a cycle of sixty was formed by running concurrently the twelve signs with ten stems, consisting of the five elements, wood, fire, earth, metal, water, each divided into an 'elder brother' and 'younger brother' to make ten.

The signs of the Zodiac were also used to indicate the points of the compass.

ASHINAGA (long legs) and TENAGA (long arms) [Pl. 25]. These creatures were reputed to be inhabitants of islands east of Shaku-sui, a 'water ladle' river, all fictions of the imagination. As they lived principally on fish, they found co-operation useful, for Long Legs would wade into the sea, carrying on his back Long Arms, who in this way was in a position to reach down deep into the water and catch the fish.

AWABI. The Sea Ear (*Haliotis tuberculata*). These open uni-valves lie deep under water sticking fast to rocks, from whence they are removed by female divers (*ama*) of great skill. They are among many shellfish used as food. Dried strips of their flesh are wrapped in folded containers called *noshi* inserted under the red and white paper string (*mizuhiki*), tied around presents. This is a polite way of indicating that the object so wrapped is a gift. The meaning of the dried fish is said to be: 'May your life be lengthened and stretched like the flesh of the Awabi.'

BAKEMONO (goblins). Many forms of these semi-human, terri-fying creatures appear in Japanese pictures and in netsuke. They should not be confused with ghosts (*yūrei*), which are distin-guished by having no feet, their bodies tapering into nothingness.

Among the most frequently depicted bakemono are:

HITOTSU-ME-KOZŌ—the one-eyed priest.

MIKOSHI NYŪDŌ—Bald-headed with lolling tongue, whose favourite amusement is looking over screens and frighten-ing people.

MITSUME-KOZŌ—Three-eyed goblin with one eye in the centre of the forehead.

ROKURO-KUBI—Whirling neck, a female goblin. On netsuke the long neck frequently slips in and out of the body.

The BAKU [Pl. 25, 4] performs a useful function, for he devours bad dreams. When visited with a terrifying nightmare the thing to do is to cry, 'O Baku! O Baku! eat my dream,' and the dream

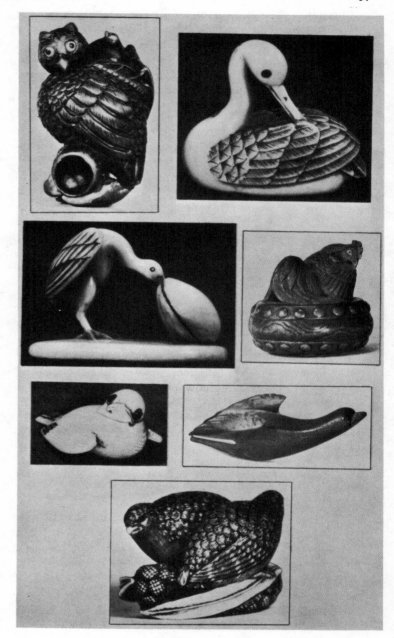

PLATE 21: BIRDS

1. Owl P. 94. *V & A*
2. Crane. *V & A*
3. The Oyster Catcher caught. B.M.
4. Cock on Drum.
5. Toy Sparrow, *fukura suzume.*
6. Wild Goose.
7. Quails and Millet.

will vanish. Perhaps it is a case of like destroying like, for the Baku itself has the resemblance of a bad dream, having a long proboscis like an elephant's trunk, tusks, a spiny backbone, a spotted hide and an ox tail. Possibly the idea was suggested by a tapir. The approach of a bad dream may be forestalled by writing on a piece of paper the character for 'baku' and placing it on or under one's pillow.

BAMBOO [Pl. 18, 3]. The part played by the bamboo in Japanese domestic economy is so extensive that many pages would be required to describe it. Suffice to say that when young it is eaten as a vegetable and when fully grown is used either in the form of a pipe, a pole, or split into strips to make a thousand and one articles in daily use. This 'grass' grows rapidly, sometimes several feet in twenty-four hours and certain varieties reach a height of twenty or twenty-five feet. Bending with the wind, it signifies pliability, and when associated with the tiger suggests security being a safe hiding place for the beast. It is one of the plants decorating the entrance of a house at the New Year.

BADGER (*Tanuki*) [Pl. 12, 3 and 4, and Pl. 23, 3 and 5]. The Japanese badger is not the animal that goes by that name in England. He is really a racoon-faced dog (*Nyctereutes procyonoides*). In folklore and superstition, he has a reputation almost as unenviable as that of the fox. Like his vulpine relative he can transform himself into human or other shape. Wrapped in a lotus leaf, he hides in lonely places, and beating his belly like a drum, lures unwary travellers to their destruction. He is sometimes shown with an enormous scrotum in which he envelops himself or beats as a drum.

BAT [Pl. 20, 3]. A symbol of good luck.

BOAR. One of the signs of the Zodiac. In the Far East he is considered an animal of outstanding courage and strength. When he is depicted with the leaves of the lespedeza, we have an emblem of power and pliability.

BONITO (*Thynnus pelanis*). A sort of tunny fish, eaten raw or dried and smoked. When shaved thin it is used as a flavouring. It is given as a present at weddings, births and other family feasts.

BUCCINUM (*Hora*). Buddhist sacred shell. In old days used by warriors as a signal horn, an emblem of victory.

BUTTERFLY, *chō* [Pl. 22, 4]. Emblem of the soul. Also a symbol of womanhood. *Sake* containers and teapots used at weddings are often decorated with butterflies.

CARP. The emblem of perseverance under difficulties, as it is supposed to ascend the stream and even leap over waterfalls. Flags in the form of carp are hung on the occasion of the Boys' Festival (5th day of the 5th month) to encourage boys to rise to fame and fortune [Pl. 20, 7].

CAT [Pl. 20, 4]. Like the badger and the fox, the cat is supposed to have the power of transforming itself into a human being, and to possess other magical powers. A geisha is sometimes called a cat because of her bewitching attractiveness. It is not a popular animal, though shopkeepers do place a carved 'beckoning cat' before their shops inviting entrance.

It is not true that all cats in Japan are of the Manx variety with short tails. Many have long ones.

CICADA [Pl. 22, 3]. In summer the woods of Japan resound with the buzzing of these beetles. So much is their music (?) appreciated that they are caught and kept in cages.

COCK [Pl. 19, 2, and Pl. 21, 4]. This bird is generally looked upon as a symbol of valour. From ancient times cock-fighting has been popular.

The cock is often depicted on a drum, and this combination is regarded as an emblem of peace, because in China a drum was beaten as a warning against invaders. In times of peace they were not required for this purpose and came to be perching places of local fowls.

In the province of Tosa there is a strange breed of cocks; the tails are ten or more feet in length. They are kept as pets and looked after with elaborate care.

CLAM (*Hamaguri*). A bivalvous mollusc the shape of which has evoked erotic allusions. A Kappa [Pl. 25, 5] or other animal caught between the valves suggests the dangers of love affairs in which escape may not be easy. Another form consists of a partly opened shell within which appears a delicately carved scene [Pl. 3, 4], such as The Palace of the Dragon King (Ryūjin), or the home of everlasting life (Hōraizan), where live the crane, the tortoise and the stag, and where grow in profusion the plum tree, the pine and the peach, all symbols of longevity.

Such scenes are called 'The Clam's Dream' and have their origin in the belief that the clam exhales a purple mist which takes the form of a mirage.

CRANE (not always clearly distinguished from heron or stork). Said to live to fabulous age, and consequently a symbol of longevity. Frequently it is the messenger or mount of one of the *Sennin* [Pl. 21, *2*].

CROW. Jimmu Tennō, the first Japanese Emperor, is said to have been guided by a large crow in his expedition of conquest. According to Chinese belief, a three-legged crow inhabits the sun.

CUCKOO (*Hototogisu*). The call of the cuckoo has been for poets the expression of unrequited love. A pet cuckoo is the subject of couplets illustrating the characters of three great generals. Nobunaga is represented as saying, 'I'll kill the cuckoo if it won't sing.' Hideyoshi expresses much the same idea by saying, 'I'll try to make the cuckoo sing.' The astute and patient Ieyasu says, 'I'll wait until the cuckoo does sing.'

DEER [Pl. 20, *5*]. An emblem of longevity because it is supposed to live to great age. When its antlers are hung with maple leaves it symbolises autumn and melancholy.

DOG [Pl. 19, *6*, and Pl. 30, *2*]. As in the case of many other animals, superstitious and popular beliefs regarding the dog are derived from China. Though in Japan the dog is looked upon as man's friend, in China he is generally regarded as his enemy. In both countries the barking of a dog is said to frighten away evil birds that endanger the lives of little children.

The dog is kept as a domestic animal and usually well treated, though one time the cruel sports of dog fighting and shooting at dogs with blunt arrows were popular.

There are many stories of this faithful servant of man. In the days of the Shogun Tsunayoshi (1681-1709), a devout Buddhist born in the year of the dog, the care of dogs was authoritatively enjoined and carried to such excessive lengths that the country groaned under their number and ubiquity.

In ancient times a special guard preceded the Emperor on his journeys barking like dogs, an idea which survives in the wearing of dog masks in the Gion festival processions and in the *haya-bito-no-mai* or dog dance.

When an infant is presented to his ancestors at the local shrine

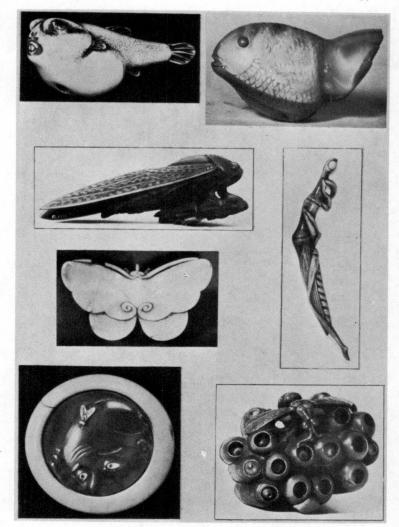

PLATE 22: FISH AND INSECTS

1. Globe Fish—*fugu*. L. 2⅛″. 2. Sea Bream—*tai*. (Mother of Pearl) L. 1⅝″.
3. Cicada—*semi*. L. 2⅛″. B.M.
4. Butterfly. 5. Praying Mantis
6. 'Drat that Fly.' (Metal repoussé work) 7. Wasps' Nest. H. 1¼″. B.M.

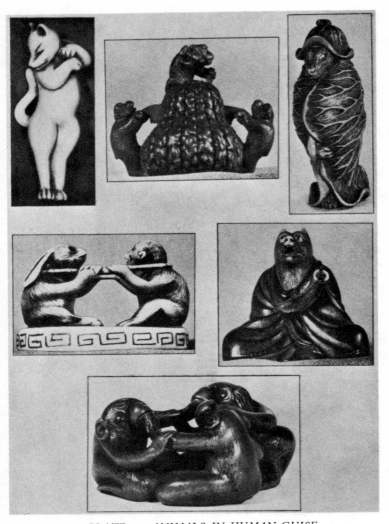

PLATE 23: ANIMALS IN HUMAN GUISE
2. Monkey Carpenters dividing a large gourd
1. Fox Dance. H. 2¾″.   3. The Wicked Badger in disguise. H.
                                            2⅛″.
4. Hare and Monkey neck wrestling.   5. The Badger as a Buddhist Priest. H.
(*kubi-hiki* or *kubi-zumō*).   1½″
6. The Three Monkeys. Speak no evil, hear no evil, see no evil. L. 2″.   B.M.

about thirty days after birth,* he receives from relatives and friends papier mâché dogs (*inu-bariko*) as emblems of good luck. They may be placed at the head of his bed to ward off evil influences.

* Miyamairi

DRAGON (*Tatsu, Ryō* or *Ryū*) [Pl. 18, *4*, and Pl. 16, *4*]. Though the dragon is well known in the mythology of many countries, the Chinese variety has a characteristic appearance peculiar to itself and differing only in small details from age to age, and in its passage from Chinese to Japanese art. Everyone is familiar with this scaly four-legged serpent with spiny back, fierce eyes, horns, long feelers and flame-like streamers at the shoulders and hind quarters. Though without wings,* it has the power of flight and can render itself invisible. It is said to be deaf [Pl. 4, *1*].

There are many forms, yellow, white, red and blue, the chief being the four, (1) the celestial dragon, the guardian of the Mansions of the Gods, (2) the spiritual dragon, which causes the winds to blow and produces rain, (3) the dragon of the earth, which marks the courses of rivers, and (4) the dragon of the hidden treasures, which protects the wealth concealed from mortals. It is one of the Signs of the Zodiac. The Buddhist deity Kwannon is represented in company with a dragon, as is also Benten, one of seven Japanese Gods of Good Luck.

The tales in which this fantastic creature appears would fill a large volume.

In China, the dragon, as the chief among beings divinely constituted, was in former times particularly symbolical of all that pertained to the Son of Heaven—the Emperor, whose throne was the dragon seat, and whose face was described as the dragon-countenance. To look upon the dragon in its entirety was said to court sudden death, and for this reason the dragon-countenance of a ruler was concealed from public gaze behind a curtain, a practice copied in the Court of Old Japan.

FOX [Pl. 20, *1*, and Pl. 23, *1*]. Among the fauna of Japan, the fox is perhaps the strangest animal of all, many marvellous tales being told of his powers and pranks. He occupies a sacred place as the guardian or messenger of Inari, the God of rice culture, to whom are dedicated countless shrines, with their conspicuous red *torii*. At either side of the entrance stands a stone fox like the Shishi or lion guardians at other temples. Within are innumerable images of foxes of varying sizes and materials, votive offerings to ensure an abundant harvest or procure one of the many favours this beneficent deity can bestow, such as the promotion or prevention of fecundity, the warding off of coughs, colds, or other ills, or the provision of wealth for the deserving. To many worshippers, it does not seem clear as to whether the fox is merely the messenger of the God, or is actually the deity Inari himself.

Unfortunately, the fox is not always the giver of good things.

* There is a form with wings.

Many are the tales of his evil exploits in assuming human form, and causing trouble and even disaster. Moreover, on occasion this strange animal can exercise such magical control over a human being that he or she, usually she, imagines that she has been turned into a fox; she speaks with a strange guttural voice and behaves like an animal. Such cases of 'fox possession' were at one time common and could be cured, it was said, by exorcism by Shinto priests. Cf. Fox Dance, p. 67 [Pl. 27, *1*].

FUJI (wistaria). Flowers of this popular creeper are much used in Japanese art. They appear in the crest of the famous Fujiwara family.

GINGKO NUTS (*Ginnan*) [Pl. 24, *5*]. The Gingko is a species of deciduous conifer often in Japan planted in temple grounds.

GLOBE FISH (*Fugu*) [Pl. 22, *1*]. Considered a delicacy, it is said that care must be exercised in preparing it for food or it may become poisonous.

HIYOKUDORI, a fabulous bird with two heads and two long tail feathers. It is a symbol of faithfulness in love.

HARE [Pl. 18, *6*, and Pl. 23, *4*]. The connection of the hare and the moon may be traced to Chinese or even Indian folklore. The Japanese see him as 'the man in the moon'. He is generally represented with a mallet beating rice in a mortar, thus making *mochi*, a word which means either a rice cake, or the full moon. Like the fox, he is said to attain great age, becoming white when he reaches his five-hundredth birthday. He is one of the signs of the Zodiac.

HŌ-Ō or HŌ. A fabulous bird of Chinese origin which appears on earth only once a thousand years at the birth of a great ruler or philosopher. To call it a phoenix is a misnomer for it resembles the bird described by Herodotus and other ancient writers neither in appearance or in character, other than in its infrequent appearance on the earth. The Chinese rank the Hō-ō among the four spiritually endowed creatures, the other three being the *Kirin*, the Tortoise and the Dragon. In Japan it is associated with branches of the *Paulownia Imperialis* (Kiri) as an emblem of imperial authority.

In appearance the Hō-ō is a combination of a pheasant and a peacock, with a cock's comb and two long tail feathers. It has rich plumage in five colours symbolical of the five virtues of

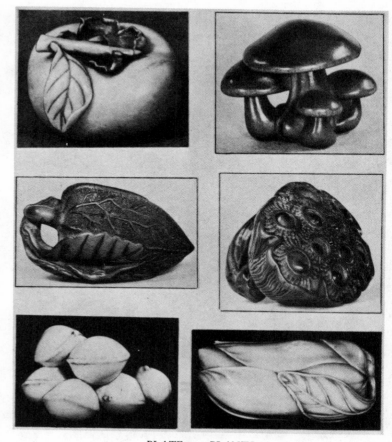

PLATE 24: PLANTS

humaneness, decency, wisdom, faithfulness and gentleness. It is also emblematic of good luck and longevity.

HORSE [Pl. 19, *1*, and Pl. 20, *2*]. Whether the horse is indigenous in Japan or not, at least he has been man's servant in the country for a very long time, for clay models of horses and their harness (*Haniwa*) have been found in tumuli dating from the 2nd Century B.C. or earlier. Among animals he seems exceptionally free from magical powers, unless it is the ability to jump out of pictures painted over-realistically.

PLATE 25: MYTHICAL CREATURES

1. Killing the *Nue*.
2. Mermaid and Child. L. 2". B.M.
3. Long Legs—*ashinaga*, and Long Arms—*tenaga*. H. 3½". B.M.
4. Baku. H. 1½".
5. Kappa. H. 1½".
6. Octopus making love to a mermaid.

KAPPA [Pl. 25, *5*]. Though the Kappa, a mythical beast, looks fearsome he is not really dangerous if properly handled. The source of his strength is, Samson-like, on the top of his head, in his case not in his hair but in a liquid that forms in a cavity in his skull. If, therefore, a Kappa should approach you in a menacing manner, the thing to do is to bow to him very politely and he, having Japanese manners, will be sure to bow in return. The consequence of this will be that the strength-giving liquid will pour out and he will thus be rendered quite harmless.

Like other beings who are too inquisitive or too bold in amorous adventures, he may find himself in a difficult position from which it is not easy to escape. This is symbolised by having his foot caught in a clam shell, a situation not infrequently depicted in the netsuke of monkeys and other animals.

The Kappa is associated with rivers and cases of drowning are attributed to his depredations. The superstitious believe that he may be appeased by throwing into a stream offerings of cucumbers for which he is said to have a taste.

In recent times, girls with bobbed hair have in slang received the sobriquet of O Kappa.

KIRI (*Paulownia imperialis*). The wood of this quick-growing tree, being very light in weight, is used to make *geta* and packing boxes. One of the crests (*mon*) of the Imperial family consists of three paulownia flowers with three leaves; the other is the sixteen petal chrysanthemum.

Similar crests were used by a number of ancient families. Cf. *Mon*, p. 112.

KIRIN (Chinese: Ki-lin) [Pl. 26, *6*]. Often called a unicorn, it bears little resemblance to our heraldic beast. True it generally has a single horn (though sometimes two, or none) but this grows not from the forehead, but from the back of the head, sloping backwards. The body is that of a deer, covered with hair, the head like that of a goat or of a horse, and the tail resembles that of an ox or of a lion. Flamelike appendages emerge from the shoulders. Buddhists claim that it treads so warily as never to crush an insect and so lightly as to leave no footprints. For virtue it has no equal and its wisdom is profound. Its appearance on earth is a happy augury.

LOBSTER. One of the emblems of longevity, it is among the objects decorating the entrance of a house at the New Year.

LOTUS (*Hasu*). The beautiful white flower of the lotus growing out of the mud is the Buddhist emblem of purity. Upon it the Buddhas sit enthroned. The root is a common article of Japanese food without, unfortunately, inducing any state of indolent luxurious enjoyment! The pod with loose seeds is a favourite subject with netsuke carvers [Pl. 24, 4].

MONKEY [Pl. 19, 3, Pl. 23, 2 and 6, and Pl. 36, 6]. The only native of Japan is the *Macacus Speciosus*, the little animal with brownish yellow fur and short tail. Baboons, apes and long-armed monkeys are for the most part copied from Chinese models. According to Taoist tradition, the monkey is the bearer of the peach of longevity and is frequently represented with this fruit.

In Japan, he is the messenger of the Shinto deity *Ō Kuni-Nushi-no-Mikoto*, being worshipped under the name of *Saru no Gongen*. He is also associated with *Koshin* or *Saruta-Hiko*, the god of the roads, and represented by the wayside Three Mystic Monkeys with paws over eyes, ears and mouth, signifying 'Neither see, hear nor speak evil'. This Buddhist injunction is a play on the words 'do not' (Zaru) and 'monkey' (Saru).

NAMAZU (the Earthquake Fish) [Pl. 26, 5]. As earthquakes are a frequent occurrence in Japan, it is not surprising that their cause should be accounted for by some superstitious belief, such as that about the *namazu*, a great subterranean cat-fish (*Silurus Japonicus*) who from time to time grows restless and wriggles. This troublesome monster is said to lie under the village of Kashima in the province of Shimōsa. In the temple grounds there is a stone, the 'pivot stone', reputed to be the centre of the earth, which in some ways acts as a restraint upon the creature's movements. We are told that in the 17th Century the Lord of Mito dug for six days to find the bottom of this stone, but in the end was compelled to abandon his effort as useless.

Another restraint on the convulsions of the monster is the rubbing of its back with a magic gourd by the deity Futsu Nushi.

NINGYO (Mermaid) [Pl. 25, 2 and 6]. The oriental variety closely resembles her European sister, but whether they are related remains a mystery. Are they both descended by a long and devious ancestry from the fish God of Chaldaeo-Babylonian religion, or have they been born of the imagination of eastern and western sailors from a distant view of gambolling seals? Who knows?

In any case, netsuke carvers have found in them an amusing subject as, for example, in Pl. 25, 6, an octopus makes love to a mermaid while she, unmoved by his devotion, fills her pipe!

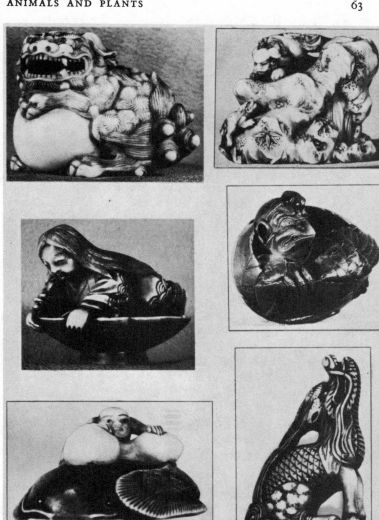

PLATE 26: MYTHICAL CREATURES
1. Shishi. H. 2″.   2. Shishi training young.
3. Shōjō.   4. Tengu.
5. Earthquake Fish, *namazu*. L. 1¼″.   6. Kirin.

NUE [Pl. 25, 1]. The Nue is a composite creature, with the head of a monkey (or of a horrible monster), the back of a badger, the feet of a tiger and the tail of a serpent. Such was the beast slain by Minamoto no Yorimasa in the year 1153 and this was how it happened. The Emperor was stricken down with some unaccountable disease and at the same time a strange 'bird' was heard singing a raucous song over the palace roof. Could there be any connection between the bird and the illness? Yorimasa determined to test the idea by shooting an arrow into the darkness in the direction from whence the uncanny noises came. The arrow hit its mark for there tumbled to earth a dreadful Nue. Ii no Hayata, the trusty retainer of Yorimasa, with great courage sprang on the monster and dispatched him. The Emperor immediately recovered and rewarded Yorimasa with the gift of a sword and the hand of a fair lady of the Court.

OCTOPUS [Pl. 25]. This product of the sea is a common article of food in Japan, though rather a tough morsel to foreigners. In folklore he is known as *Umi Bōzu*, the priest of the sea, suggested perhaps by the resemblance of his smooth belly to the shaven head of a priest. Inconsistent with this role, however, is his character, which is extremely amorous as is expressed by the firmness of his embrace. He is associated with *Ryū-Jin*, the Dragon King of the Sea, and appears as an attribute of the Dragon King's Messenger.

OWL (*fukuro*) [Pl. 21, 1]. The owl is said to be an emblem of ingratitude, but, on the principle of like curing like, is also considered to be a talisman against ingratitude.

SEA BREAM (*tai*) [Pl. 22, 2]. A popular delicacy at Japanese feasts, it is eaten raw or cooked. Ebisu, one of the Gods of Good Luck, is seldom portrayed without a tai.

SHISHI (lion) or KARA SHISHI (Chinese lion) [Pl. 26, 1, 2]. The *shishi* with his curly mane, glaring eyes and large mouth, bears little resemblance to the king of beasts as we know him. There being no lions in Japan or indeed in ancient China, artists had to rely on travellers' tales or crude pictures and in the course of time there evolved the conventionalised form to be seen in Chinese and Japanese art. In both countries pairs of these animals carved in stone guard the entrances of temples, one with open mouth said to be uttering the first Sanscrit vowel Aum, and the other with mouth closed saying Um, the last letter of the alphabet, signifying the beginning and end of life. They are also said to

represent the Yin and Yang, the male and female, active and passive principles of Chinese Philosophy. One may have a large ball, the sacred jewel in his paws, with perhaps a small ball in his mouth. The Shishi is sometimes called a Korean Dog or Dog of Fo.

Shishi are in art associated with waterfalls and peonies. They train their young in strength and fortitude by hurling them down steep rocks.

For LION DANCES, see p. 67.

SHŌJŌ [Pl. 26, 3]. A mythical creature who lives by the sea shore and is inordinately fond of *sake*. Its long red hair is said to provide a valuable dye!

SNAIL [Pl. 20, 6]. The snail is said to be a symbol of the impermanence of worldly power.

SANSUKUMI. This triad of the snake, the toad and the snail symbolises the practice of checking and counter-checking one another. The snake devours the toad, and the toad the snail, while the slime of the snail is believed to be death to the snake.

SPARROW (*Suzume*) [Pl. 21, 5]. The sparrow is said to be an emblem of friendship and of the industry of the farmer. The Sparrow Dance, immortalised by the pictures in Hokusai's Mangwa, has been copied in netsuke. A conventionalised form known as the inflated sparrow (*Fukura Suzume*) is common. In this shape it is a popular children's toy. Cf. The Tongue Cut Sparrow, p. 42.

TENGU [Pl. 26, 4]. These mythical inhabitants of the forests are depicted in two forms, the human-shaped *konoha tengu* with an inordinately long nose, sometimes confused with Saruta Hiko no Mikoto, a Shinto deity, and the other the bird-like Tengu, called a *karasu tengu* (Crow Tengu). A common subject in netsuke is a *Tengu* being hatched from an egg. Often they wear a tiny cap, like an *Eboshi*.

WILD GOOSE (*kari*) [Pl. 21, 6]. Japanese history contains a number of battle stories in which the wild goose plays a part. For example, one night in A.D. 1180 when the Minamoto General Takeda no Yoshinobu was reconnoitring with a small band of six hundred men, a flock of wild geese was aroused. The Taira forces numbering eighty thousand, frightened by the clamour, thought they were being outflanked and fled in confusion.

7

Dances, Musical Instruments and Games

DANCES

DANCING, WHICH HAS always been popular in Japan, takes many forms from the slow and solemn movements of the religious or classical dance, to the gay abandon of the village festival [Pl. 27, 4, and Pl. 27, 5]. The technique differs widely from that of the West. The waving of hands and arms and the rhythmic swaying of the body are the main features. Legs and feet play a subordinate role. There is no display of the lower limbs or 'high kicks', which would be quite impossible with the costumes worn. There are two words for dance *mai* and *odori*, the former generally applied to ancient dances, though there is no strict rule. Some story is almost always illustrated or suggested by the dance and miming is frequent.

KAGURA, the Sacred Dance. In primitive times dancing was, as in most countries, an act of worship performed to please the Gods and to ensure bountiful harvests. The origin of the Kagura is reputed to be the dance of Uzume, whereby she inveigled the Sun Goddess from her retreat in a cave, though the mythological account of this performance (see pp. 50-51) does not suggest any solemn sanctity. Throughout the centuries, the dancing of the Kagura has been a feature of the festivals of Shinto shrines, and on many occasions throughout the year at the great shrines of Ise and Nara.

GIGAKU, Ancient Dances. This term, which signifies a 'theatrical performance with music', is the generic word applied to ancient dances, which include *Dengaku* (Peasant Dances), *Bugaku* (Court Dances) [Pl. 28, 2], and *Sarugaku* (Monkey or Comic Dances).

BUGAKU. These dances were introduced from China about the year A.D. 200. After a long period of disuse, they came into fashion again at the beginning of the 19th Century. Originally they were the pastime of the aristocracy who themselves performed them in their palaces and temples on state occasions accompanied by complicated melodies played on drums, flutes and the *shō*. The conductor of the orchestra played the big drum! Later, rich families began to employ professionals. Large masks were worn, often completely covering the head.

RAN-RYŌ-MAI [Pl. 28, 2] was one of the many types of Bugaku. It was performed by a single dancer at athletic gatherings, wrestling matches and archery contests. He wore a huge mask, in expression terribly fierce, with a movable jaw showing enormous teeth or tusks. On the top of the mask was a dragon spitting fire. A small gold baton was carried.

DENGAKU. A religious pantomime, accompanied by songs, performed by itinerant priests, travelling from district to district. Originally it was a peasant dance, the word Dengaku meaning 'Dance of the Rice-fields'. It flourished in the 12th Century, when the priest artists drew inspiration from the stirring events

PLATE 27: DANCES

1. Fox Dance.   B.M.
2. Nō Dancer. The Dragon King's Messenger. L. 2″.   B.M.
3. Sambasō. H. 1⅝″.
4. Village Dance. H. 1⅞″.   B.M.
5. Itinerant Street Dancers, *manzai*.
6. Butterfly Dance.

of the day, but also introduced accounts of their own valorous deeds.

SARUGAKU (monkey music). An ancient comic dance reputed to be Chinese in origin. It became popular in the Kamakura era and little by little took the form of historic drama, thus preparing the way for the lyrical Nō dances. The comic element was a forerunner of the Kyōgen, the interludes introduced to afford comic relief to the long-drawn-out Nō.

NŌ or NŌGAKU [Pl. 27, 2]. The various forms of dance, court, peasant, comic and itinerant, which had delighted and amused the Japanese from earliest times, paved the way for the rise in the 14th Century of the great lyrical dramas, known as Nō. Nō is said to have sprung from the efforts of Zen priests to inculcate religious ideas and develop the sentiment of piety. For this purpose they chose or invented tales portraying the woes and sufferings of humanity, first historical and legendary, and later incidents of everyday life. In Tokugawa times certain Nō actors were supported by the Government and their offices became hereditary. Also, many feudal lords and great families patronised Nō performers, providing private stages for the displays. There was no scenery, the stage being about sixteen feet square, open on three sides, covered with a roof, with the fourth side decorated by an old pine tree. Masks were worn by the principal performers and the costumes were elaborate and colourful. Female parts were taken by men. An orchestra and choir supplied the music and chanted the story. The repertoire was varied and large, as many as two hundred and fifty having been listed.

SAMBASŌ [Pl. 27, 3]. An ancient dance performed as a 'curtain-raiser' before the main part of the programme began. Originally it was a Nō dance but was afterwards transferred to the Kabuki, or popular theatre. It was propitiatory in character, to appease the gods and make them indulgent for any inadvertent errors that might occur in the dances that followed. There were two dancers, both wearing masks representing an old man (*okina*) one black with white spots or tufts of hair, the other white with black spots and tufts. Their clothes were decorated with pine trees and storks and other emblems of longevity. They carried in their hands a fan and a rattle.

A Sambasō dancer is easily distinguished by the long mitre-like cap he wears with a red spot representing the sun and twelve stripes signifying the twelve months.

There is a tradition that Sambasō was first performed as a

religious act when the people of Nara were terrified by fire and smoke which issued from a hole in the earth in the year A.D. 808.

SHISHIODORI OR MAI (lion dance). This dance was performed in the streets at the New Year. The chief dancer wore a large mask resembling a Shishi with a movable jaw and a cloth at the back to hide the body. Nowadays such masks are made as toys with which boys like to think they can frighten their parents or friends. Kappore and Shakkyō were also 'lion' dances, but performed with Nō dances or on the stage.

SHIRA-BYO-SHI. A dance with this name was at one time performed by girls going from town to town and from house to house. Its chief characteristic was the costume worn, white (*shira* means white) with large sleeves and red trousers. Though the dancers carried two swords they wore no armour. They sang chivalrous and romantic songs.

BON ODORI [Pl. 27, 4]. This is the most famous of dances performed by the peasants themselves. The occasion is the Feast of the Dead in the middle of July, when the souls of the departed are believed to return to their old haunts. To welcome them houses and streets are decorated with lanterns and this is why it is sometimes called 'The Feast of Lanterns'. Fairs are held with amusements, acrobatics and fireworks. In the evenings the villagers gather in the temple courts or other open spaces to dance. The participants form a circle and follow each other around, singing and waving towels or handkerchiefs. The custom has for the most part disappeared in towns, but survives in remote villages.

MANZAI. An ancient dance originally performed exclusively at the Imperial Court. In later ages it became the characteristic dance of certain poor comedians who wandered about the country performing it, especially at the New Year. They went in pairs, the principal dancer waving a fan and crying '*Manzai*', i.e. 'Ten thousand years' or 'Long Life', while his companion beat time on a hand drum [Pl. 27, 5].

KITSUNE ODORI, fox dance [Pl. 27, 1], in which the performers simulate foxes by letting their hands hang to look like paws.

SPARROW DANCE, in which the dancers, wearing broad hats, wave their sleeves to imitate sparrows' wings. This dance is illustrated in Hokusai's *Mangwa*.

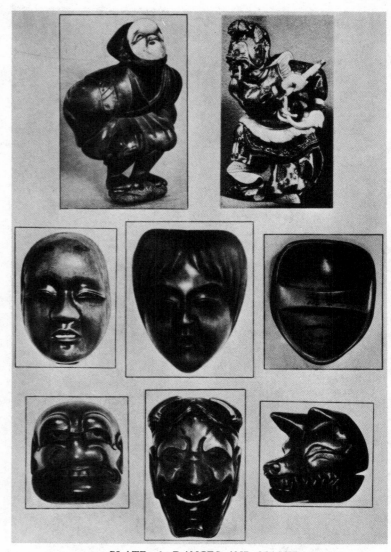

PLATE 28: DANCES AND MASKS

1. Comic Dance, *kyōgen*.   2. Ancient Court Dance, *ran-ryō-mai*.

NETSUKE MASKS

1. Young Woman with false eyebrows (*bobo-mayuge*)   2. Wine loving Sprite, *shōjō*   3. Back of mask, with bridge for cord
4. 'Anger'   5. Female Demon, *hannya*   6. Kyōgen Mask. Fox with articulated jaw

PLATE 29: MUSICAL INSTRUMENTS
1. Pellet Bell—*Suzu*.   2. Mokkin.
3. Tsuzumi.   4. Samisen.
5. Koto. L. 3½″.   B.M.
6. Sho.   7. Mokugyo. L. 2⅛″.   *V & A*

BUTTERFLY DANCE [Pl. 27, *6*].   A woman's dance in which butterfly wings are attached to the shoulders.

KYŌGEN [Pl. 28, *1*].   Comic interludes between the serious Nō dances.

MUSICAL INSTRUMENTS

Musical instruments are frequently depicted in netsuke, either by themselves or in the hands of a performer.   There are many varieties in each class of wind, strings and percussion, the following being a few of the more important types.

It is hardly necessary to say that in carvings of this sort absolutely accurate representation is not to be expected.

FUE (flute) [Pl. 8, *4*] is a term which includes two forms of flute, that which is played from the end (pipe) and that held across the mouth like the modern western flute, and called by the Japanese *yokobue*, or 'side-blowing flute'.   The former type is claimed to have originated in Japan and to be the instrument frequently referred to in native mythology and the chronicles of early times, whereas the latter came from China.   Japanese flutes are made of bamboo, with the interior lacquered red.

The SHAKUHACHI [Pl. 36, *5*] resembles a recorder.   It is made of thick bamboo, lacquered inside.   Well played it is one of the sweetest and mellowest of wind instruments.   It is specially associated with the *Komusō*.

SHŌ NO FUE.   A very ancient instrument composed of twenty-two pipes arranged side by side like 'pipes of Pan'.

SHŌ [Pl. 29, *6*].   This is composed of a compact bundle of seventeen thin bamboo reeds fixed into a circular lacquer wind chamber of cherry wood or hard pine, the air passing in a channel round the central support.   It is fitted with a silver mouthpiece. Similar instruments are found in many parts of South-east Asia.

KOTO.   The Koto is the aristocrat of Japanese musical instruments, not only because it has found favour with women (and men) in the highest social circles, but also because, beyond any other, it is capable of producing music more elaborate in form, deeper in emotional content, and more beautiful in its harp-like sounds. It is the instrument of the amateur as much as of the professional musician. Known as the Kin in China, where its use has been traced back to very ancient times, it was introduced into Japan about the 7th Century A.D. In both countries it has often been altered and improved, yet nevertheless maintaining its essential characteristics. "Like the Kin, the Koto is fantastically supposed to be a dragon, symbolical of all that is noble and precious, lying on the sea-shore, holding such sweet converse with the waves that angels came to sit and listen by his side'★ [Pl. 29, 5].

A typical modern Koto consists of a sound box about 6 feet long, 9½ inches wide and 3 to 5½ inches deep. There are 13 strings made of tightly twisted silk cord soaked in wax, stretched over separate bridges which are placed at various intervals. The player sits on the floor facing the middle of the long side and plucks the strings with small ivory plectra, attached by stalls to the tips of the thumb, the first and second fingers. Other effects are produced with the other fingers or by depressing the strings to alter the pitch. Much music has been composed in recent times for this instrument.

SAMISEN (or *Shamisen*) [Pl. 29, 4], which resembles a banjo, with three strings, but played with a large plectrum, is the popular instrument of Geisha, the leading instrument in the theatre and in later forms of the Nō dance. It probably originated in China, travelling thence to the Loo Choo islands and from there to Japan. A famous philosopher at the beginning of the 18th Century said: 'The samisen stirs up what is evil in us. Its smallest sound evokes more evil in our hearts than any other instrument is able to do.'

TEMPLE BELLS [Pl. 10, *1*, and Pl. 13, *3*]. 'The tsuri-gane (suspended bell) of Japan gives forth a voice of the most exquisite sweetness and harmony—a voice that enhances the lovely landscapes and seascapes, across which the sweet solemn notes come floating in autumn evenings and in the stillness of summer's noon-day hazes. The song of these bells can never be forgotten by those who have once heard it.'★ One reason for this soft sweetness is that the bell is not struck by a metal clapper, metal against metal, but by a large beam hung horizontally and swung so that the end strikes the outside of the bell. Some of these bells are of enormous size, that of the Chion-in in Kyoto, cast in 1633, being ten feet, ten

★ Sir Francis Piggott, *The Music and Musical Instruments of Japan*, page 37.

★ *Japan, Its History and Art*, by Captain F. Brinkly, Vol. VII, p. 99.

PLATE 30: CHILDREN

1. Child in Chinese dress, *karako*   *2.* Playing with puppy. H. 1½″
3. Daruma on drum. H. 1½″.   *4.* In bath. H. 1¼″
V & A
5. Mocking Gesture, *bekkanko*. H. 1¼″.   *6.* Playing at Lucky Temple Pillar, Nara.
     B.M.   H. 1½″. *V & A*

PLATE 31: DOMESTIC LIFE

1. Domestic scene. H. 1⅜″.   *B.M.*   2. Fulling Cloth on block, *kinuta.*
3. Fireplace with Coverlet, *kotatsu.* L. 1½″.   4. Disappointed Rat Catcher. H. 1½″.
     B.M.   *B.M.*
5. Beating Clothes in Mortar. *V & A*   6. Making Mochi.

inches high, nine feet in diameter, and weighing forty-three tons. The oldest is that of Tōdaiji Nara, cast in A.D. 732 and weighing forty-nine tons. The largest bell in the world in actual use is one in Moscow weighing one hundred and twenty-eight tons. Big Ben only weighs about thirteen and a half tons.

SUZU (pellet bell) [Pl. 29, *1*]. In contrast with these monsters, there is the Suzu which is like the European horse harness bell, spherical, with a narrow slit at the bottom and a loose ball inside. In remote times they were attached to a rattle used in the Kagura —sacred dances—and more recently in the Sambasō dance of the Kabuki theatre. In medieval days they were mounted on rings on the hilts of swords; they were attached to the talons of falcons and the necks of pet dogs. To-day very small children have them fastened in their *geta* (clogs). A larger form is hung at the entrance of Shinto temples, especially those of *Inari* the Fox God, and rung by shaking a rope, to call the attention of the deity.

A priest cleaning an enormous *suzu* is a symbol of perseverance and the desire for perfection [Pl. 29, *1*].

The MOKKIN [Pl. 29, *2*] has thirteen wooden tablets in a frame and resembles a xylophone. It is played with two sticks.

BIWA [Pl. 14, *4*], resembles a mandolin, having four frets less than half an inch in breadth at intervals on the neck. Different notes are produced by varying the pressure above the frets. The strings are struck with a large plectrum, which is also sometimes used to beat the body of the instrument. A form known as the *satsuma biwa* is used to accompany heroic recitations and ancient songs of love and war, the chief being the famous *Heike-Mono-gatari* which tells of the conflict between the Heike and Genji clans in the 12th Century.

DRUMS. There are three forms of drum: (1) plain cylindrical drums, (2) those with braces or cords, and (3) those of dumb-bell shape called *tsuzumi* [Pl. 29, *3*]. Large drums are suspended in a frame. A smaller form rests in a frame and is played with two sticks. The *tsuzumi* is held in the left hand over the left shoulder and is played with the right hand.

GONGS are of many forms:

MOKUGYO (wooden fish) [Pl. 29, *7*]. An earlier form of the

instrument resembled a fish and hence the name. It is a wooden gong, struck with a padded stick and is an accompaniment to worship in Buddhist temples. Apparently the hollow note caught the fancy of a western dance musician as it is to-day frequently found in Jazz orchestras, being called 'A temple block'.

DŌBACHI ('copper cup'), is a soft and sweet-sounding gong, in the form of a large bowl resting on a cushion on top of a lacquered stand. It is struck with a leather-covered stick and provides an accompaniment to Buddhist worship.

GAMES

BEKKANKO [Pl. 30, 5]. Mocking gesture of pulling down the lower eyelid—'see my eye'.

DAKYŪ, a kind of polo introduced from China in the 6th Century A.D. There are fourteen players. The balls are not hit but scooped up with sticks something like long lacrosse sticks and placed in a netted bag.

HANETSUKI. Battledore and shuttlecock, played by girls at the New Year.

KAKUREMBŌ [Pl. 33, 4]. Hide and seek.

KEMARI. Kick-ball or football, introduced from China in the early 7th Century A.D. Quite different from the football of the West. The ball must be kept in the air by repeated kicks.

KŌTORO KOTORO (Catch the Child). The players form a line holding each other's backs with the 'father' at the head, who attempts to manœuvre his family so that the end child may not be caught by the odd child out called an *oni* or demon.

SHŌGI (Chess) in its Japanese form is the game much like Western chess, which the less educated prefer to *go*. Like our game each side has a row of pawns in front and at the back a row of those of higher rank with a king in the centre. The movements of the pieces are similar, though the Japanese game has complications peculiar to itself.

GO [Pl. 33, 6] is a game corresponding to chess in the West in the intelligence and skill which it evokes. It is played on a

PLATE 32: CUSTOMS

1. Jō and Uba. H. 1¼″.   B.M.   2. Standing Doll, *tatebina*. H. 3″. B.M.
3. Exorcising Demons, *oni yarai*. H. 1⅜″.   4. Tea Ceremony, *cha-no-yu*. B.M.

5. Medicinal blister, Moxa.   6. Festival of the Seven Herbs, *nanakusa*.

PLATE 33: GAMES

1. Wrestling, *sumō*.
3. Art of Self Defence, *judō*.
5. Hobby Horses

2. Children at Play
4. Hide and Seek, *kakurembō*.
6. Go.

square, heavy wooden board, marked with nineteen straight lines each way, crossing at right angles and thus making three hundred and sixty-one points of intersection. There are one hundred and eighty white and one hundred and eighty-one black markers (called *ishi* or stones) which the players in turn place on the crossings (not on the squares) and the object of the game is to occupy more space than one's opponent. When a group of markers are surrounded they are removed and the space becomes the property of the one who has achieved the encirclement. There are many complications. The game is reputed to have been introduced to Japan from China in the 8th Century.

MEKAKUSHI.   Blind-man's buff.

SUGOROKU.   A game of progress along one of the great highways, like 'Snakes and Ladders'.

KEN.   Games played with the fists and fingers. A group of players hold their clenched fists and at a signal fling out their fingers in different forms. The two most popular forms are:

> JANKEN, in which the fore and middle fingers represent scissors, the hand held flat, paper, and the clenched fist, a stone. Scissors cut and therefore conquer paper, paper wraps stone, and stone breaks scissors.

> KITSUNE KEN (Fox ken). In this three positions represent a fox, a hunter and the headman of the village.

SUMŌ [Pl. 33, *1*] and JŪDŌ [Pl. 33, *3*]. There are two entirely different forms of wrestling in Japan, Sumō and Jūdō or Jūjitsu, the kind better known in the West. Sumō is never anything but a game whereas Jūdō, though now practised as a sport, was originally for the purpose of acquiring the art of self defence even if this led to serious injury or death for an opponent. Young men often wrestle in Sumō fashion for fun, but there is no doubt that the great popularity of the sport in Japan is associated with the performances of the professional wrestlers (*Sumōtori*).

In comparison with the western athlete, the Japanese sumōtori presents a strange appearance, being fat, indeed excessively fat, for weight counts for something in this game. Yet in spite of his handicap, he trains himself to be not only strong but agile. The ring is about twenty-four feet in diameter, surrounded by straw rice bags, filled with sand, and surmounted by a canopy on four pillars. The victor is the one who can throw his opponent or push him out of the circle, conforming to intricate rules, for the observance of which an umpire, fan in hand, dodges about the ring. On entering the arena, the protagonists, naked except for a loin cloth and belt with tassels, wash their mouths and scatter salt in accordance with a traditional ceremony of purification. Then, after limbering up, they stoop down, with clenched fists on the ground and glare at each other for some moments, until suddenly they spring together like tigers on their prey. The bout may be over in a moment, or the umpire may decide on a technicality that there must be another trial.

In Japanese history the earliest forms of wrestling were hardly more than rough-and-tumble fights, such as that in the reign of the Emperor Suinin (24 B.C.) when Nomi no Sukune overthrew and killed a braggart by kicking him and breaking his bones.

By the 8th Century, when official wrestling parties were held in the Imperial Court, Sumō had developed into a sport with rules and formalities. In the days of Yoritomo, the first Shogun (d. 1199) annual wrestling parties formed part of the festival at the Hachiman shrine. About this time one friendly match started a train of events with dire consequences. One of the contestants, Sukeyasu of Kawazu, picked up his opponent, Kagehisa, by the loin cloth and gave him a violent throw, known ever since as the 'Kawazu throw'. So enraged was Kagehisa, that, forgetting all rules of sport he sought to slay Sukeyasu and, indeed, later succeeded with the help of an accomplice. This in turn led to the famous vendetta of the Soga brothers, p.40.

All medieval wrestlers were soldiers and could not be called professionals in the modern sense of the word. It was not until some three hundred years ago that the sport reached its modern phase of professionalism. This began with performances to raise funds for building Shinto shrines or Buddhist temples. After the Restoration in 1868 the Great Wrestling Association was formed and Sumō became the highly commercialised sport of the day.

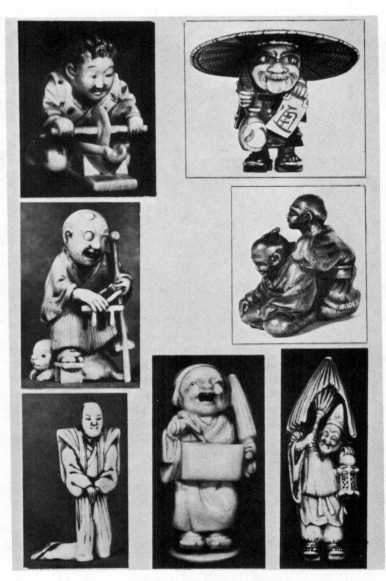

PLATE 34: OCCUPATIONS

1. Druggist with Mortar, *yagen*
3. Blind Masseur, *amma*. H. 1½″. B.M.
5. Courtier. H. 1⅝″. B.M.
6. Umbrella Mender. B.M.
2. Sake Vendor. H. 1½″. V & A
4. Massage. H. 1½″. B.M.
7. Temple Watchman. H. 3½″. V & A

8

Activities, Objects, etc.

AMMA [Pl. 34, *3* and *4*]. The blind masseur formerly known as a shampooer. In ancient Japan blindness was very prevalent by reason of the excessive incidence of smallpox, purulent opthalmia and to a lesser extent syphilis. Blind men were, however, usually able to earn a good living as masseurs or musicians. After examination masseurs were admitted into a sort of guild which classed them as long-robed persons, in company with priests, doctors and diviners. Their profession was often so lucrative that they became money lenders. As money lenders are not as a rule popular this may account for the somewhat unkind humour with which their misfortunes are depicted by netsuke carvers. For some curious reason their bald or shaven heads are nearly always disfigured by a wen.

Massage is widely practised not only for the cure of bodily ailments, but also to soothe and restore tired and aching limbs at the end of a hard day's work.

CHA-NO-YU (the tea ceremony) [Pl. 32, *4*]. This institution, considered by some as an embodiment of the highest culture in art and taste, has a long history. It is believed to have originated in the practice of monks of the Zen sect of Buddhism, who drank tea to keep themselves awake during their long periods of meditation. By the 14th Century, however, tea parties had become occasions of luxurious display and frivolous amusement. Towards the close of the 15th Century, the Shogun Yoshimasa abdicated his throne to devote himself to refined pleasures in his gorgeous palace of Ginkakuji in Kyoto, and with the help of two Buddhist abbots evolved certain rules for the ceremonial consumption of tea, which still hold good. The main characteristics were and still are an appreciation of articles of antiquity and a regard for simplicity in the performance of the rite. A century later, under the great Hideyoshi, an enthusiastic follower of the cult, the various 'schools' which had sprung up were unified and the ceremonies codified by the famous tea master Sen-no-Rikyū, who gave the ceremony the principles and rules of etiquette that have never varied since. When properly carried out the proceeding should take place in a small rustic room, nine feet square, built for the purpose. After a preliminary meal, the guests, four or five in number, are invited to enter this room through a low doorway. A small quantity of powdered tea is put into the tea bowl which is used on these occasions, and hot water (not boiling) is poured upon it. With a bamboo whisk the host beats it into a frothy mixture. The bowl is then handed to the guest at the head of the row who takes three sips, showing appreciation by the noise he makes in sucking, and then a half, or little sip. After wiping the brim carefully he hands the bowl to the next guest, who repeats the three and a half sips, and so on down the line. The empty bowl is handed back to the host who washes it and prepares a cup for each guest separately. 'The bare procedure is simple,' says a Japanese writer, 'but the complexity lies in the hard-and-fast rules to be observed in the arrangement of the room, and respecting the utensils to be used, and the manner in which they should be handled in making tea, the way the tea should be drunk, the number and style of bowls and salutations to be made in offering, receiving and returning the bowls, and also in the instructions, as to when and how the bowls and other articles in the room are to be taken up and admired, and the manner of expressing such admiration and replying thereto.'* To the uninitiated, it all seems very tedious, but it is hardly likely to have had so many devotees over so many years of Japanese history, if its practitioners did not believe that the discipline had a value in character building, in inculcating good manners and that there was some aesthetic satisfaction in the performance itself.

DOMESTIC SCENE [Pl. 31, 1]. The man and his wife are sitting beside a *hibachi*, or charcoal fire box, over which they can warm their fingers or warm a kettle for tea. Here a stew is being cooked and the wife is pouring out *sake* for which the husband holds a tiny cup, the *sake* having been warmed. The posture is the ordinary one of kneeling down and then sitting back on the heels. There are no chairs in a Japanese house.

DUTCHMEN [Pl. 37, 1]. Dutchmen with long coats and large hats are frequently depicted in netsuke. They often carry a dog or a cock, the latter suggesting that cock-fighting was one of their favourite sports.

When Japan was hermetically closed to intercourse with the outside world in the middle of the 17th Century, the only exception made was a small trading post in the tiny island of Deshima at Nagasaki. Here for two hundred years dwelt half a dozen or so traders from Holland who, though suffering somewhat ignominious treatment, managed to maintain a profitable business of imports and exports. Glass, velvet, woollen fabrics, clocks, telescopes and firearms were imported, paid for by the export of silks, pottery, gold and copper. A few scientific investigators like Kaempfer (1690) and Siebold (1823) visited Deshima and were able to tell the West something of this strange secluded country. On the other hand, some Japanese in spite of the stringent laws against any fellowship with foreigners, managed to learn Dutch and acquire some knowledge of the scientific progress of the West. The elements of mathematics, geography, botany and, most important of all, medicine were surreptitiously

* *Home Life in Tokyo*, by Jukichi Inouye.

PLATE 35: OCCUPATIONS

1. Fishmonger (see back view Pl. 4, 2.) H. 1½″. B.M.
2. Falconer. H. 1¾″. B.M.
3. Girl Diver, *ama*. H. 3″.
4. Cooper. H. 1½″. V & A
5. Cormorant Fisher. B.M.
6. Potter. H. 1¼″. B.M.

studied with diligence.   Indications of this infiltration of Western knowledge are to be found in the netsuke depicting firearms [Pl. 39, *6*], compasses, telescopes [Pl. 39, *4*, *7*], etc.

FANS.   From earliest times fans have been used in Japan both by men and women.   There were many varieties, the chief being the round fan incapable of being shut (*uchiwa*), the folding fan (*ōgi*) and the metal fan (*gunsen*) used by officers of higher ranks in directing their forces.   The Japanese claim that the folding fan was a native invention, borrowed by the Chinese in the Ming dynasty (1386-1644).   Fans were used not only for comfort in hot weather, but as bellows, as trays on which things were handed, and as accessories of dancers and storytellers.   A notable fan was the one decorated with a red sun which the Taira Lady Tamamushi hoisted on the prow of her boat in the battle of Yashima, 1185. Yoshitsune, observing the challenge, commanded a famous archer Munetaka Nasu no Yoichi to shoot it down. This he did, directing his arrow with such skill that it hit the pin of the fan.

JŌ AND UBA, OR TAKASAGO [Pl. 32, *1*].   This old couple are the Darby and Joan of Japan, emblematic of long life, happiness and conjugal fidelity.   The legend is that they are the personification of two ancient pine trees near the village of Takasago on the beautiful pine-clad coast of the Inland Sea, of which Japanese poets have never ceased to sing.   Here this happy couple spent their days, the man with a rake, his wife with a broom, sweeping up the pine needles.   Often, as in the illustration, they are accompanied by the crane and tortoise, symbols of longevity. Their effigy is displayed at wedding feasts together with a Shimadai (p. 78).

KOTATSU [Pl. 31, *3*].   A foot-warmer with a quilt over it.   No provision is made for heating a Japanese house, which is cold and draughty in winter.   Even in Tokyo there may be ten degrees of frost and in the mountains it is much colder.   The chief protection is thicker clothing.   A common device, however, is a *kotatsu*.   Into a square hole cut in the floor a box is sunk filled with ashes in the centre of which burns a small charcoal fire. Over the hole is placed a rack about fifteen inches high and over the rack is spread a quilt.   The family sit round this with their feet under the quilt enjoying the warmth which comes up through their clothing.

PLATE 36: OCCUPATIONS

1. Pedlar. H. 1¾″   *2.* Mirror Polisher. H. 1¼″.
                                                 V & A
3. Making a Millstone. *B.M.*   *4.* Acrobat. H. 1½″. *B.M.*
5. Itinerant Flute Player, *komusō.*   *6.* Monkey Showman, *sarumawashi.*
B.M.

MIRROR [Pl. 36, *2*], a man polishing a mirror in the shape of the character for 'heart', suggesting the necessity of keeping the mind clear.

Mirrors were made of metal, generally bronze, the surface coated with tin and quicksilver, and highly polished. They were circular in shape with a straight handle and the back adorned in relief with flowers, birds or Chinese characters. Mirrors are among the objects found in prehistoric sepulchral mounds. A mirror was used to entice the Sun Goddess from her retreat. There is a pretty story of a woman who, when dying, told her young daughter to look in the mirror she bequeathed when she wanted to remember her mother. The father married again and the stepmother was upset seeing the child continually looking in the mirror, supposing that the child must be practising black magic against her. She therefore asked her husband to get rid of the child. However, when the story of the dying wish was explained the stepmother relented and all was well.

MOCHI [Pl. 31, *6*]. Special glutinous rice steamed and beaten in a wooden mortar into a smooth sticky paste. This is made into cakes and dried. Large round flat cakes are called *kagami mochi* (mirror mochi) from their resemblance in form to ancient mirrors and are offered singly or in tiers to the gods, to be consumed afterwards by the priests or worshippers. To make them edible, the cakes are cut in slices and toasted or boiled.

Mochi is considered a great delicacy and is eaten in quantities at the New Year and on other festive occasions.

Small cakes, called *dango*, are also made.

MON. A badge borne by the nobility, their retainers, and Samurai to denote the family to which they belonged, or in whose service they were enrolled. To-day there is no restriction upon their use and people of all classes may be seen with them in the five traditional places on Japanese dress. The mon is usually called a crest, though it differed in many respects from the Western heraldic device of that name. When it began to be used is unknown but the general opinion is that it became general during the civil wars of the 12th Century. Much ingenuity has been displayed in making a vast number of simple designs.

NANAKUSA [Pl. 32, *6*]. The feast of the Seven Herbs of Spring. On the seventh day of the first month the head of the house put on his best clothes (*kami-shimo*) and with somewhat elaborate ceremonial prepared a thick soup of the seven herbs of spring,

PLATE 37: FOREIGNERS

1. Dutchman.	*2.* Chinaman	*3.* European
4. Blackman with Coral	*5.* Egg Tester. H. 2½″.	*6.* European
kurombō	*V & A*	

parsley and six other edible herbs. Drinking this concoction was said to ensure good health during the coming year. The custom of eating food made with the seven herbs survives in parts of Japan, but shorn of the ancient ceremonial.

In addition to the Seven Herbs of Spring, there are Seven Herbs of Autumn, which are admired for their beauty but not eaten.

MOXA [Pl. 32, 5]. Blistering certain spots on the body was a cure frequently used in olden days. The downy covering of the dried leaves of the plant *Artemisia Moxa* was made into a sort of cone, which was placed on the skin and lighted, thus producing a blister. There were certain recognised places on the body where this might be done, avoiding a ligament or proximity to a bone, where serious harm might result.

SARUMAWASHI [Pl. 36, 6]. A showman who travels about the country entertaining children with a performing monkey. The monkey has a predilection for peaches with which he is often associated in art.

SHIMADAI. A tray on legs on which are a miniature pine, bamboo and plum tree, together with the emblems of longevity, the tortoise and the crane. The evergreen pine signifies longevity, the pliant bamboo gentleness,and the plum which blossoms while the snow is on the ground, suggests fidelity in adversity. This ornament, together with the Takasago or Darby and Joan (p. 76), is displayed at a wedding feast.

SKELETONS. The macabre, often treated with humour, had the same kind of vogue that is often to be found in European art of medieval days. The skeletons were usually crudely executed and in most cases the idea conveyed was that of a spirit or ghost rather than of a realistic representation. For example, the skeleton beating a *mokugyo* represented a departed priest [Pl. 38, 2]. Sometimes, no doubt, they were 'memento mori' to suggest the Buddhist lesson of the brevity and uncertainty of life.

SKULLS [Pl. 38, 1 and 4], to be used as netsuke were necessarily modified in design by suppressing or bending in the processes and projections to prevent their catching in the clothes. Occasionally these netsuke are found beautifully carved with accurate anatomical details, but were probably intended to show the

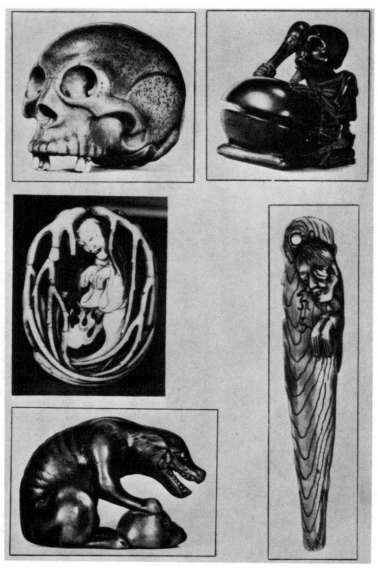

PLATE 38: MACABRE

1. Skull.
3. Ghost
4. Wolf with Skull. H. 1½"
2. Departed Priest at his devotions. H. 1½".
5. Ghost of Oiwa. (*Sashi Netsuke*).

ingenuity of the carver rather than for actual use. The same may be said of skulls with movable jaws.

TANABATA. A popular festival observed on the seventh day of the seventh month (lunar calendar) when the stars Vega, the Weaving Princess, and Aquila, the Divine Herdsman, are in conjunction in the Milky Way, the River of Heaven.

The meeting of the separated lovers is an occasion for writing poems.

TINDER BOXES. These mechanical tinder boxes, precursors of the modern cigarette lighter, were of Japanese origin and unknown elsewhere [Pl. 39, 1, 2].

'There can be no doubt that this remarkable locket-like form of the tinder-pistol originated in the ingenuity of some clever Japanese workman, who, chancing to obtain a European flint-lock pistol, copied its pistol-action with remarkable accuracy, though on a diminutive scale, enclosing the whole in an imitation of a walnut-shell'.*

The earliest specimens date from the 17th Century.

YAGEN (mortar for grinding drugs) [Pl. 34, 1]. It was made of iron or bronze shaped like a boat, the drugs being pulverised by a wheel with a handle through the axis, which was rolled to and fro.

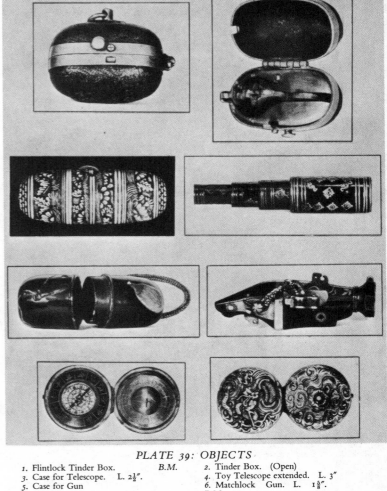

PLATE 39: OBJECTS

1. Flintlock Tinder Box.   B.M.
2. Tinder Box.   (Open)
3. Case for Telescope.   L. 2½".
4. Toy Telescope extended.   L. 3"
5. Case for Gun
6. Matchlock Gun.   L. 1⅝".
   B.M.
7. Compass and Sundial.   H. 2¼"
8. Cover of Compass and Sundial.   Silver. (Open)

* Catalogue of Bryant and May Collection in the Science Museum, South Kensington.

PRONUNCIATION OF JAPANESE WORDS

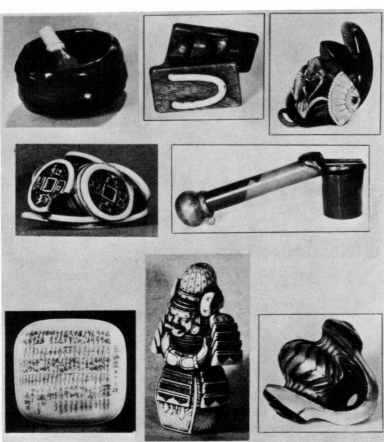

Vowels as in Italian that is (approximately)

a as in father
e ,, ,, men
i ,, ,, police
o ,, ,, for
u ,, ,, bush
ai as 'y' in my
ei as the 'ay' in may
au as the 'ow' in cow

Vowels marked long are slightly prolonged as in Latin. Consonants as in English, but 'g' never has 'j' sound. Double consonants are slightly emphasised.

NAMES

Japanese usage in names is highly complicated and differs widely from occidental practice. The following is a rough guide:

1. *Kabane* or *Sei*, the ancient and aristocratic family or clan name, e.g. Minamoto, Fujiwara.
2. *Uji* or *Myōji*, surname, before 1870 only used by gentry.
3. *Zoku* or *Tsūshō*, common name like our Christian name, e.g. Gentarō, Jirō, Saburō.
4. *Nanori* or *Jitsumyō*, resembles our Christian name. Anciently it was used in combination with the Kabane, e.g. Minamoto no *Yoritomo*.
5. *Yōmyō*, boy's infant name, e.g. Ushiwaka, the Yōmyō of Yoshitsune. It was changed to the Jitsumyō in the Gembuku ceremony at the age of fifteen.
6. *Azana*, nickname.
7. *Gō*, pseudonym or art name. Most netsuke carvers are known by their Gō, e.g. Shūzan, Gyokusai.
8. *Geimyo*, stage name of singers, dancers, actors, e.g. Danjūro.
9. *Okurina*, posthumous, honorific name applied to Emperors, e.g. Jimmu, Meiji.
10. *Hōmyo* or *Kaimyō*, posthumous name inscribed on Buddhist memorial tablets.
11. *Yobi na*, girl's personal name, often preceded by honorific 'O', e.g. O Kiku.

PLATE 40: OBJECTS

1. Tea Cup, *chawan*, and whisk, *chasen*, for Tea Ceremony. P. 108
2. Clogs, *geta*
3. Court Head-dress, *oikake kammuri*
4. Cash. L. 2″. *V & A*
5. Portable Writing Case, *yatate*
6. Inscriptions of 53 Stations on the Tokaido
7. Suit of Armour
8. Real Shell. Silver Mounted

GLOSSARY

of Japanese Words used in Books on Netsuke, Sales Catalogues, etc.

ABURA: oil
ABURA-AGE: fried bean curd
ABURA-AKAGO: a child licking oil
AKAGANE: copper
AMA: fisher girl, diver
AMADO: wooden sliding shutters
AMARYŌ: rain dragon
AMIGASA: braided hat
AMMA: blind masseur
ANDON: night-light
ANKA: foot-warmer
AOI: hollyhock
ASA: hemp
ASA-NO-HA: hemp leaf
ASAGAO: morning glory
ASHINAGA: Mythical creature with long legs
AWABI: sea ear
AZANA: nickname

BAKEMONO: goblin
BAKU: mythical animal
BAKUFU: shogunal council
BEKKAKO or BEKKANKO: mocking action of pulling down the lower eyelid
BETTŌ: groom
BINRŌJI: betel nut
BIWA: musical instrument like a mandolin
BŌBŌ-MAYUGE: painted spots on forehead
BOKUDŌ: herd boy
BOKUSHA: itinerant fortune-teller
BOKUTŌ: wooden dummy sword
BON: tray
BON MATSURI: festival of the dead
BON-ODORI: dance at festival of the dead
BOSATSU: Buddhist saint

BŌZU or BONZE: Buddhist priest
BUGAKU: ancient court dance
BUMBUKU: lucky
BUSHI: ancient name of military class
BUTSU: Buddha
BUTSUDAN: household Buddhist shrine

CHA: tea
CHA-NO-YU: tea ceremony
CHAGAMA: tea kettle
CHA-IRE: tea jar
CHAJIN: master of the tea ceremony
CHASEN: whisk used in tea ceremony
CHATSUBO: tea jar
CHAWAN: teacup
CHIDORI: plover
CHIKARA-ISHI: large stone used for competition in strength
CHŌCHIN: paper lantern
CHŌCHŌ: butterfly
CHŌCHŌ-ODORI: butterfly dance
CHŌZU-BACHI: tank for washing hands near a privy.

DAIBUTSU: large image of Buddha
DAIDAI: bitter orange
DAIJINGŪ: Temple of the Sun Goddess
DAIKON: radish
DAKYŪ: game like polo
DOHYŌ: wrestling ring
DOHYŌ-IN: position assumed by a wrestler

EBI: prawn
EBOSHI: ancient form of cap
EJI: yeoman of the guard

EKIBYŌ or EKIREI: epidemic
EKIREI NO SUZU: bell giving warning of epidemic

FUCHI-GASHIRA: pommel
FUDE: writing brush
FUDE-KAKE: writing brush rest
FUDE-ZUTSU: holder for writing brush
FUE: flute or pipe
FUGU: globe fish
FUJI: wistaria
FUKIN: napkin
FUKIN-IRE: napkin-holder
FUKUJUSŌ: plant, the Pheasant's Eye
FUKUSUKE: toy in the shape of a dwarf with a large head
FUKURA SUZUME: toy sparrow
FUNDOSHI: loin-cloth
FUROSHIKI: cloth for wrapping parcels
FUTATSU-DOMOE: symbol of two commas, former flag of Korea
FUTON: quilt
FUSUMA (KARAKAMI): sliding partition

GAKI: hungry ghost
GEISHA: professional female dancer, singer and entertainer
GEMBUKU: name-changing ceremony of a boy at about the age of fifteen
GETA: wooden clog
GINNAN: gingko nut
GO: game
GOBAN: board on which Go is played

GOHEI: sacred strips of paper or cloth
GOHEI-KATSUGI: Gohei carrier
GOMOKU-NARABE: game played on a Go board, 'gobang'
GOZEN: female title—Lady
GYŌJA: person who goes about performing religious austerities

HABŌKI: feather brush
HAGI: Lespedeza
HAGOROMO: feather robe
HAIFUKI: bamboo ash-pot
HAKAMA: wide trousers worn by both sexes
HAKO: box
HAKUTAKU: horned shishi, unicorn
HAMAGURI: clam
HANA: flower
HANAGASA: hats worn by geisha at festivals
HANA-IKE: flower vase
HANIWA: clay image
HANNYA: female demon
HARI: needle
HARIGANE: wire
HASHI: chopsticks
HASHI-IRE: chopstick case
HASU: lotus
HATO: dove
HATOBUE or HATOFUE: pigeon whistle
HAYA-BITO-NO-MAI: dog dance
HIBACHI: vessel for charcoal fire
HIBASHI: chopsticks for tending a fire
HIFUKI: fire blower
HIME: princess
HIMONO: dried fish
HIMOTŌSHI: holes for cord

81

HINA-MATSURI: doll's festival, March 3rd

HINOKI: conifer, cypress

HIRAGANA: cursive form of forty-seven syllable phonetic writing

HITOTSU-ME: goblin with one eye

HIUCHI-BAKO: tinder box, metal mechanical tinder box used as netsuke

HIUCHI-BUKURO: bag to hold flint, steel and tinder

HIYOKU-DORI: mythical bird with double tail

HŌGEN: honorific title given to some priests and artists

HŌ-Ō: mythical bird, sometimes called a phoenix

HŌ-Ō: retired emperor become monk

HORA: trumpet shell

HORAIZAN: home of everlasting life

HORO: hood

HŌSHU-NO-TAMA: Buddhist emblem

HOSSU: priest's brush of long white hair

HOTOTOGISU: cuckoo

HŌZUKI: winter cherry

HYŌSHIGI: striking blocks

HYŌTAN: gourd

ICHIMOKU: one-eyed goblin

ICHIRAKU: woven with wire or rattan

ICHŌ: maidenhair tree

IHAI: wooden memorial tablet

INGYŌ: seal

INRO: medicine case

INU-BARIKO: dog-shaped box given by a woman to her friends after Miyamairi (p.88); also used for paper handkerchiefs

ISHI-DORO: stone lantern

ITTŌBORI: rough carving with few strokes (Hida School).

JAKAGO: bamboo basket filled with stones and used for building embankments

JANKEN: game

JIGOKU: hell

JINJA: Shinto shrine, also called Miya

JIZO-GURUMA: prayer wheel

JORŌ: low-type prostitute

JU: character for 'long life'

JŪBAKO: nest of boxes

JUI: Chinese word for sceptre held by Buddhist priests (Japanese Nyo-i) an attribute of Fukurokuju

KACHI-KACHI: tick tick, crackling

KAGAMI: mirror

KAGAMI-BUTA: netsuke with metal disc

KAGAMI-MOCHI: flat rice cake used as a sacred offering

KAGO: small palanquin

KAGURA: sacred dance

KAI: shell

KAIRAI: puppet

KAIRAISHI: itinerant puppet showman

KAISHO: print-style writing

KAKEMONO: hanging scroll

KAKI: persimmon

KAKI: oyster

KAKIHAN: written seal or artist's mark

KAKU: angle

KAKUTAN: form of unicorn like a pig

KAMA: iron pot, oven.

KAMABOKO: boiled fish paste

KAMADO: stove

KAMI: God, Shinto deity

KAMI-SHIMO: old ceremonial dress

KAMURO: little girl employed in a brothel

KANA: syllabic writing

KANABŌ: iron rod, or club

KANAMONO: metalware

KANAE: kettle

KANJINCHŌ: account book

KANNUSHI: Shinto priest

KANZASHI: ornamental hairpin

KAPPA: mythical creature

KARAKAMI (FUSUMA): sliding door

KARAKO: Chinese boy or boy in Chinese dress

KARAKUSA: arabesque

KARASHISHI: Chinese lion, Dog of Fo

KASA: umbrella

KASA: straw hat

KATABAMI: wood sorrel

KATABORI: statuette carving

KATAKANA: square form of syllabic writing

KATAKIRI: engraved lines variable in depth and thickness as in handwriting

KATANA: long and slightly curved sword

KAYAKU-IRE: gunpowder bag

KEBORI: hairline engraving

KEN: short straight sword

KESHŌ-MAWASHI: ornamental apron

KEYAKI: Zelkova tree

KIKU: Chrysanthemum

KIMONO: dress

KINCHAKU: purse of brocade or leather

KINJI: gilt letters

KINUTA: stand on which cloth is beaten for cleaning

KIRI: pawlonia tree

KIRIN: unicorn

KISERU: tobacco pipe

KISERU-ZUTSU: a pipe case; sheath of wood, ivory or leather

KITSUNE: fox

KITSUNE-BI: foxfire, will-o'-the-wisp

KITSUNE-TSUKI: fox possession, a mental derangement

KITSUNE NO YOMEIRI: foxes' wedding, a demon's lantern march

KOBAN: ancient gold coin

KOBITO: dwarf with a large head

KOCHŌ: butterfly

KOCHŌ-NO-MAI: butterfly dance

KŌGŌ: incense burner

KOI: carp

KŌJIN: God of the kitchen

KOKORO: heart

KOKU: measure of rice, about five bushels

KOKUTAN: ebony

KOMUSŌ: Samurai turned mendicant priest, plays flute, head covered with basket

KORO: gourd

KOSHI-SAGE: article hung from girdle

KOTATSU: foot-warmer

KOTO: musical instrument

KŌTORO-KOTORO: child's game

KUBI-HIKI: neck wrestling

KUBI-ZUMŌ: neck wrestling

KUCHI-NASHI: cape Jasmine (juice used for staining netsuke)

KUDAN: fabulous animal who always tells the truth! Has head of a man, body of a bull, three eyes on its flank and horns on its back

KUN: Japanese pronunciation of a character

KUMADE: bamboo rake

KURIKATA: moulding

KUROMBŌ: black man

KURUMI: walnut

KUSA: grass

KUSAZURI: tassets of armour

KUSAZURI-BIKI: tussle with tassets

KYŌGEN: comic dance

MAGATAMA: ancient ornament in form of a comma

MAGO-NO-TE: back scraper

MAKIE: gold lacquer

MAKIMONO: rolled scroll

MAKKIN: gilding

MAKURA: pillow

MAMORI-FUDA: charm or amulet

MANJI: swastika

MANJŪ: round cake

MANJŪ-NETSUKE: netsuke in form of above

MANZAI: dance by itinerant performers at New Year

MARISHIKI: decorated ball

MARUBORI: carving in the round

MATSURI: religious festival

MEGANE: spectacles

MEKAKE: concubine

ME-TSUBUSHI: pepper blower

MI: seed or fruit

MIKO: girl who serves a shrine, witch

MIKOSHI: sacred palanquin

MIKOSHI-NIUDO: three-eyed goblin

MIKOTO: title applied to Shinto deities, 'augustness'

MIKUJI: divining sticks

MIKUJI-BAKO: divination box with rods

MINO: straw raincoat

MINOGAME: turtle with tail

MISO: fermented beans

MITSUDOMOE: symbol consisting of three commas

MITSUME: goblin with long tongue and three eyes

MIZUHIKI: red and white, or gold and silver string for tying up presents

MIZUSASHI: water jug used in tea ceremony

MO: duckweed

MOCHI: cake made of pounded, glutinous rice

MOKKIN: musical instrument

MOKKO: oblong-shaped basket

MOKUGYO: wooden gong used in Buddhist temples

MOMIJI: maple

MOMIJI-GARI: excursion to see maple trees in autumn

MON: crest

MOXA: plant used in blistering for medicinal purposes

MUKADE: centipede

MUSUBI: knot

NAGINATA: halbert

NAMAKO: trepang or sea slug

NAMAZU: earthquake fish

NANAKO: twilled silk cloth

NANAKUSA: Festival of Seven Herbs

NARUKO: clapper

NASHI: pear

NASHIJI: lacquer with gold and silver dust

NASUBI: egg plant

NATAMAME: horse or sword bean

NEMBUTSU: Buddhist prayer

NENGŌ: year period

NINGYŌ: doll

NINGYO: mermaid

NINSOKU: coolie

NIŌ: two Deva kings guarding temple gates

NIOI-BIN: scent bottle

NŌ: lyric drama or dance

NOSHI: folded paper with dried fish enclosed, given with presents

NUE: mythical creature

NYORAI: Buddha

OBI: sash or girdle

ŌGI: folding fan

ŌHARAME: woman of village of Ōhara

OIBANE: battledore and shuttlecock

OIKAKE: noble's cap with ear-pieces

OIRAN: high-class prostitute

OJIME: bead used on strings to attach netsuke

OKIMONO: ornament

OKINA: old man

OMINAESHI: patrinia scabio-saefolia

ON: Sino-Japanese pronunciation of a character

ONI: demon

ONI-NO-NEMBUTSU: demon praying to Buddha

ONI-YARAI: driving out demons with beans at the New Year, (Lunar Calendar)

OTAFUKU: 'big breasts', irreverent name for Okame.

RAKAN: Buddhist saint

RAMMA: transom, fanlight

REISHI: lichi

RENKON: lotus root

ROKURO: lathe, potter's wheel, pulley

ROKURO-KUBI: goblin with long neck

RŌNIN: masterless samurai

SAGEMONO: 'hanging things', articles hung from girdle

SAISHIKI: water colour

SAISHIKI-NETSUKE: coloured netsuke

SAKAKI: Cleyera Japonica, sacred Shinto tree

SAKAZUKI: wine cup

SAKE: rice wine

SAKURA: cherry

SAMBŌ-KŌJIN: kitchen gods with three faces and four hands

SAME: shark

SAMISEN: musical instrument like banjo with three strings

SAMURAI: member of military class

SAN-SUKUMI: group of frog, snake and snail

SARU: monkey

SARUMAWASHI: monkey showman

SASHI: rod netsuke

SEMBEI: wafer

SEMI: cicada

SENNIN: hermit magician, immortal

SENSEI: teacher or master

SENTOKU: alloy of brass, tin and lead

SHAKU: mace, baton

SHAKUDŌ: alloy of copper and gold

SHAKUHACHI: musical instrument like a recorder

SHAKUJŌ: a priest's staff

SHARI: residue of human remains like a small piece of gum found in ashes of a cremated saint.

SHARITŌ: reliquary

SHIBAYAMA: form of decoration

SHIBUI or SHIBUMI: astringent, in good taste

SHIBUICHI: alloy of silver and copper

SHIBU-UCHIWA: tanned round fan

SHICHI-FUKU-JIN: Seven Gods of Good Luck

SHIME-KAZARI: New Year's decoration at house entrance

SHIMENAWA: sacred straw rope with paper strips (gohei) attached

SHINOBU-GUSA: hare's foot fern

SHINZO: newly-made courtesan, young wife

SHIOFUKI: type of mask

SHIOHI-GARI: shell-gathering at low tide

SHIPPŌ: enamel

SHIPPŌ-YAKI: cloisonné

SHISHI: Chinese lion, dog of Fo

SHISHI-ODORI or SHISHI-MAI: lion dance

SHITAN: red sandalwood

SHŌ: musical instrument

SHŌ-CHIKU-BAI: combination of pine, bamboo and plum

SHŌGI: Japanese chess

SHŌGUN, general, commander-in-chief, military ruler of the country

SHŌJI: window or door sashes with paper panes

SHŌJŌ: drunken sprite

SHURO: hand-warmer

SŌJŌBŌ: the Tengu King

SOROBAN: abacus

SOTOBA: grave post with symbols of the five elements, ether, air, fire, water and earth

SUGOROKU: a game

SUIGARA-AKE: ash tray

SUISEN: daffodil

SUKASHI-BORI: openwork carving

SUMI: Indian ink

SUMI: charcoal

SUMI-TSUBO: ink pot

SUMŌ: wrestling

SUMŌTORI: professional wrestler

SURIBACHI: earthenware mortar (for making bean soup)

SURIBAKO: box for writing materials

SURIKOGI: wooden pestle (for making bean soup)

SURIMONO: printed matter, greetings cards

SUSUKI: kind of pampas grass

SUZU: pellet bell

SUZUME: sparrow

TABAKO-IRE: tobacco pouch

TAI: sea bream

TAIKO: large drum

TAKAMAKIYE: raised gold lacquer

TAKARA-BUNE: treasure ship

TAKARAMONO: treasures

TAKASAGO: Nō play of Jo and Uba

TAKE: bamboo

TAKE-GASA: bamboo hat

TAKE-NO-KO: bamboo shoots

TAKO: octopus

TAKO-TSUBO: pot for catching octopus

TAMA: jewel

TANABATA: Festival of the weaving princess and the Divine Herdsman, 7th day of the 7th month

TANGO-NO-SEKKU: Boy's Festival, 5th day of the 5th month

TANUKI: badger, racoon dog

TASUKI: cord for holding back sleeves when working

TATAMI: straw mat

TATE-BINA: a type of doll

TATE-EBOSHI: form of cap

TAWASHI: scrubbing brush

TEBORI: hand carving

TENAGA: mythical being with long arms

TENGU: mythical creature of the woods

TENNIN: Buddhist angel

TENNŌ: The Emperor

TENSHI: 'Son of Heaven', the Emperor

TENSHO: seal characters

TENUGUI: hand towel

TEPPATSU: begging bowl, iron bowl

TETSU-GAI: gunpowder flask

TŌBORI: 18th-century carving in Chinese style

TŌFU: bean curd

TOKKO: Buddhist symbol

TOKONOMA: alcove where ornaments are placed and scrolls hung

TONKOTSU: bulky wooden tobacco pouch

TORI: bird

TORII: Shinto gate

TORI-MOCHI-IRE: bird-lime holder

TŌRŌ: lantern

TOORI AKUMA: winged goblin

TSUBA: sword guard

TSUGE: boxwood

TSUISHU: red lacquer thickly applied and carved

TSUITATE: single leaf screen

TSUTA: ivy

TSUTSUMI: hand drum

UBUME: goblin

UCHIWA: round fan

UGUISU: Japanese nightingale

UKI-BORI: carving in relief or embossed

UMI-BŌZU: goblin priest of the sea

UROKO: imbricate pattern

USHI DŌJI: herd-boy symbolising 'perfect calm'

WANI-GUCHI: wooden gong suspended before a Shinto shrine
WARABI: bracken
WARAJI: straw sandal
WARA-ZUTO: straw bale

YABUKŌJI: spear flower

YAGEN: druggist's mortar
YAKURŌ: medicine chest
YAMABUSHI: itinerant monk
YAMA-UBA: mountain witch
YANEBUNE: covered boat
YATATE: portable case for writing materials

YUBI-ZUMO: hand wrestling
YUKATA: nightdress
YUKI-ONNA: goblin
YŪREI: ghost

ZABUTON: cushion

ZŌGAN: inlay
ZŌGE: ivory
ZŌRI: form of sandal
ZUKIN: women's winter headgear

BIBLIOGRAPHY

Sōken Kishō (in Japanese). By Inaba Michitatsu (Tsuriu). Osaka, 1781.

Netsuke no Kenkyū (*The Study of Netsuke*). By Ueda Reikichi. Osaka, 1943. New edition, 1952. (In Japanese.)

Netsuke (in German). By Albert Edward Brockhaus. Leipsig.

Netsuke. By F. M. Jonas, London: Kegan Paul, 1928.

Netsuke, a Miniature Art of Japan. By Yuzuru Okada. Tokyo: Japan Travel Bureau, 1951.

Netsuke (in Swedish and English). By Stig Roth. Goteborg, 1933.

The Art of the Netsuke Carver. By Frederick Meinertzhagen. London: Kegan Paul & Routledge, 1956.

The Animal in Far Eastern Art, and especially in the Art of the Japanese Netsuke. By T. Volker. Leiden: E. J. Brill, 1950.

Koji-Hoten (in French). By C. Weber, *Dictionary of Japanese & Chinese Art*, 2 Vols. Published by the Author, Paris, 1923.

Legend in Japanese Art. By Henri L. Joly, London: John Lane, 1908.

Pointers and Clues to The Subjects of Chinese and Japanese Art. By Will H. Edmunds. London: Sampson Low, Marston & Co. Ltd., 1934.

Japan, its History, Arts and Literature, Vol. VII. By Capt. F. Brinkley. Boston and Tokyo: J. B. Millet & Co., 1902.

Descriptive and Historical Catalogue of Japanese and Chinese Paintings in the British Museum. By William Anderson. British Museum, London.

Historical and Geographical Dictionary of Japan. By E. Papinot. Tokyo, 1910. Lithoprint 1948.

Handbook for Travellers in Japan. By Basil Hall Chamberlain, F.R.G.S., and W. B. Mason. London: John Murray, 6th Edition, 1901.

Things Japanese. By Basil Hall Chamberlain, 4th Edition. London: John Murray, 1902.

Home Life in Tokio. By Juichi Inouye. Tokio Printing Co., 1910.

Weird Tales of Old Japan. By Eisaburo Kusano. Tokyo News Service, 1953.

Tales of Old Japan. By Lord Redesdale. London: Macmillan & Co., 1908. (First Edition 1871.)

Myths & Legends of Japan. By F. H. Davis. London: George G. Harrap & Co., 1912.

We Japanese. By Frederick De Garis. Published by Miyanoshita Hotel, Japan.

Japanese Treasure Tales. By Kumasaki Tomita and G. Ambrose Lee. London, Osaka: Yamanaka & Co.

Fairy Tales from Far Japan. By Susan Ballard. London: R.T.S., Second Ed., 1909.

The Japanese Fairy Book. By Yei Theodora Ozaki. London: Constable & Co., New Edition, 1922.

Romances of Old Japan. By Yei Theodora Ozaki. London: Simpkin, Marshall, Hamilton, Kent & Co., 1919.

The Mikado's Empire. By William Elliot Griffis. New York: Harper & Brothers, Fifth Edition, 1886.

Chinese Biographical Dictionary. By Herbert A. Giles. London: Bernard Quaritch, 1898.

Short History of Japan. By A. L. Sadler. London: Sydney, 1946.

History of Japan. By James Murdock and Longford. 3 Vols. London: Kobe, 1903, 1910, 1926.

Japanese Names and how to read Them. By Koop and Inada. London: Bernard Quaritch, 1923.

Transactions of the Japan Society of London. Vol. III 1893-5: *The Evolution of the Netsuke*. By Marcus B. Huish. Vol. V, 1898-1901: *On Certain traces of Evolution noticed in Japanese Art*. By Walter L. Behrens.

Catalogue of Harry Seymour Trower Collection. Edited by H. L. Joly. Glendining, 1913.

Catalogue of Walter Lionel Behrens Collection, Part I, Netsuke. By Glendining.

Catalogue of Tomkinson Collection.

MAGAZINE ARTICLES

The Art of Collecting Netsuke. By Edward Gilbertson. London: Studio, II, No. 10, p. 123. 1894.

Netsuke. Their Makers, Use and Meaning. By Trower H. Seymour. Magazine of Arts, 1889.

Netsuke Stories. By Rev. Lionel B. Cholmondeley. London: Connoisseur, July 1914, June 1924, April 1925.

INDEX